SACRED
HEART

D1114201

SACRED
HEART

Gateway to God

Wendy M. Wright

ORBIS BOOKS

Maryknoll, New York 10545

Founded in 1970, Orbis Books endeavors to publish works that enlighten the mind, nourish the spirit, and challenge the conscience. The publishing arm of the Maryknoll Fathers and Brothers, Orbis seeks to explore the global dimensions of the Christian faith and mission, to invite dialogue with diverse cultures and religious traditions, and to serve the cause of reconciliation and peace. The books published reflect the views of their authors and do not represent the official position of the Society. To learn more about Maryknoll and Orbis Books, please visit our website at www.maryknoll.org.

Published by Orbis Books, Maryknoll, New York, U.S.A.
Manuscript editing and typesetting by Joan Weber Laflamme.

Library of Congress Cataloging-in-Publication Data

Wright, Wendy M.
    Sacred Heart : gateway to God / Wendy M. Wright
      p. cm.
    Includes bibliographical references.
    ISBN 1-57075-389-X
    1. Sacred Heart, Devotion to. I. Title

BX2157 .W75 2001
232—dc21

2001041420

Contents

List of Illustrations

Preface

He is standing above me, back angled and arms outstretched to grasp my small, upraised hands. We are, respectively, calf and waist high in a saltwater tide pool and the bright glare of the midday Southern California sun has caused me to turn my face sideways and peer, squint-eyed, at an indeterminate point to the left of the camera's lens. His gaze is focused squarely on me. I could not be more than two years old. That would make him thirty-nine: a slender, agile thirty-nine year old in drawstring swim trunks, eyes gentle and attentive as they rest on his little girl.

This book is about the Sacred Heart. Or, better, it is a meandering, rummaging response to an intellectual obsession that has haunted me for the better part of a dozen years. Pinpointing its origin is difficult. On the most obvious level, my fascination with the Sacred Heart devotion, both as visual imagery and as a visionary manifestation, grows naturally out of my academic specialty. Francis de Sales and Jane de Chantal, the early-seventeenth-century co-founders of the monastic community of the Visitation, were the focus of my dissertation. Later in the seventeenth century a Visitation nun, Margaret Mary Alacoque, received a series of revelations of the Sacred Heart. It makes sense that as the years have progressed I have "moved up" the Grand Siècle chronologically and come to focus on the Sacred Heart revelations with which the Visitation is most notably associated.

But the obsession has less obvious roots as well. Long convinced that theological reflection is more an art form than a science, I have been drawn to consider the role of beauty in spiritual formation and to ponder the role of the arts in the religious enterprise. These themes no doubt have always been alive for me, but the year 1994 marked a definitive turn in that direction. For some time the specifics of my academic work had felt eviscerated. Whatever compelling energies had propelled me through graduate school and into professional academia had evaporated. The simpatico, indeed, the deep identity I had experienced with St. Francis and St. Jane, had disappeared. Where to next?

The answer came in 1994 on the rhododendron-lined driveway of my parents' Santa Barbara home. We had buried my father the previous day. The door to the workshop stood ajar. There in his retirement my father had fashioned papier-mâché sculptures, pressed handmade papers into fanciful shapes, and plied his calligrapher's artistry. There too were the goldsmith tools and machinery—awls, steel files, buffers, soldering guns—that had been his during his decades as an artist whose media were gold, silver, and gems.

The gifts of visual artistry that were my father's had leap-frogged a generation. Now I see those gifts again in the oil paintings and intaglio prints my eldest daughter creates and in the sure eye and flawless line of my son's cartooning. As for myself, under my parents' flowering rhododendrons, I knew what should come next. It had to do with the intersections between art, especially visual art, and religion. I needed to understand that. Hence the image of the Sacred Heart.

With me that afternoon was the director of my doctoral committee. He had come to sit at the early morning memorial held in Quaker silent meeting fashion. Now he stood on the driveway of my parents' home and listened attentively as I stammered out my attempt to articulate "what comes next." This man was my "Doktorvater," to use the term academics employ to describe the intense filial relation between a master teacher and student. And it was through him that I had grown into my own authority as a scholar, writer, and teacher. It had not been so much the subject matter we had shared—although in fact we had waded for the first time together into the currents of Christian mysticism, he from the shores of historical theology, I springing off the dock with the enthusiasm of a scholarly neophyte—it was the shared sense of life's poignant, pregnant mystery that most bonded us. It was his grand, rhetorical questions flung into the air between us—on a carpool ride between university and home, in an elevator between classes, across phone lines, on the backs of napkins discovered early morning in my mailbox—that teased me into intellectual adulthood. It was his playful, offhanded wrestling with issues serious and sober that taught me to advance boldly into questions most people despair of or leave to the experts. It was, most of all, his fascination with Beauty as a focus of academic and existential concern that drew me into and out of myself. For at the core of religion it is Beauty who beckons. She is the face of that never-sated restlessness that goads us on to God.

My own father had no patience with institutional religion. A long-time peace activist and associate of the secularized, though Quaker-founded, American Friends Service Committee, he regarded rigid religious dogmatism as the primary root of violence and the cause of most of the insanity that the human race had heretofore perpetrated. When my adolescent peers were turning their conservative parents' hair gray with their unkempt clothing, hippie paraphernalia, and anti-Vietnam protests, I, from my counter-cultural "upper middle-class Bohemian" social strata, was stretching my own independent wings by frequenting Catholic churches and reading in as yet to be widely discovered Christian mystical literature. In becoming a Catholic in my late twenties I left my father's world behind. In a sense, then, in 1994 the trajectory of the independent self was tracing itself into a completed circle with the realization that in the next chapter art and religion had to meet and kiss.

There is another, less obvious, level on which my obsession with the Sacred Heart can be discovered. At its root is the personal, and quite private, question: Who is this Jesus? This Christ? I hesitate even to inscribe the words, recalling the exasperated impatience of a friend—a Methodist woman pastor—as she railed against a third woman colleague: "How can she call herself a Christian if she can say she just doesn't get the 'Jesus thing'?" In a sense, I don't "get it" either. I admire and am capable of discoursing intelligently on the "historical Jesus" with whom my social-ethicist husband so identifies. I can teach an eloquent class on the myriad ways Christians have conceptualized the role and person of Jesus the Christ over their two millennia of institutional life. And I've written passionately and persuasively of the lives of historic women and men who have surrendered all they have and are to follow that Jesus. But sometimes I wince inwardly when I find myself listed in the column headed by the title "Christian." On these occasions I can dodge deftly behind the label "Catholic" until the logical implication unfolds: Catholics are Christians. No doubt I shrink inwardly at the title partly because of the way the term *Christian* is so heavily freighted in American discourse today. Certainly there is a feminist piece to my discomfort as well. How can a male savior save women? This is a question with which I have grappled.

Perhaps I should simply alleviate my anxiety once and for all by describing my theology as theocentric rather than Christocentric. But the Jesus question is, for me, essentially other than this. The truth of the matter is that somewhere along the way I lost Jesus. My young adult conversion to the Roman Catholic Church skirted around the issue. It was Mary—Madonna, Queen of Heaven, Mediatrix, Second Eve, Virgin-Mother—and the saints—those impassioned pray-ers who thirsted for a life larger than life—who drew me in then. Perhaps I can describe it the way my mother describes the visual condition from which she suffers: macular degeneration. The eye is unable to see with its center, its macular. Peripheral sight, which becomes enhanced, is all that remains of vision. For me, it is as though for over twenty-five years I've been operating primarily on peripheral eyesight. The Sacred Heart, it seems, is my way of reclaiming central vision—of seeing Jesus—at least as it encompasses the Christian faith.

I should remark that part of my problem with the figure of Jesus has been my instinctive, and probably theologically sound, aversion to the "tritheism" that pervades the Western church. For centuries we have tended to speak and proceed as if God—the Father, Son, and Holy Spirit—is three distinct entities rather than a Trinity. Either we strip the historical Jesus of his aura of divinity or we adore a godlike phantom free-floating above the human condition. Or we envision a literal father who victimizes the son whom we view as a separate individual. Or we want to know what a man who lived two thousand years ago in Palestine would do when we face ethical problems that only humans living in the technological nightmare that is the twenty-first century could have created. I have never been able to separate Jesus from my sense of God present as Spirit or from God who transcends categories, affirmations, analysis, and apprehension.

Still, there was once a time when those possible tritheistic distinctions were not yet conscious and I *knew* Jesus. This knowing spanned my grade school years and converges with the time I spent as a junior choir member at Hollywood First Presbyterian Church. Jesus was then an intimate, experienced as tangibly present just behind my left shoulder. He was not connected to the preaching of the church. The fiery sermons of the head pastor made little impression on me as I daydreamed in the choir loft between hymns. My parents, who never joined the church or allowed me to join, but who drove me to choir (because it was the best musical training in the city for a youngster) and who attended only on choir festival days, made me vaguely aware of the preaching only because they complained bitterly of it.

Instead, Jesus was alive in the hymns. He was alive in the lift of breath and soaring of voice: "Unfold, unfold, unfold ye portals everlasting!" Alive in the poignant lilt of melody: "Christ when a child, a garden made." Alive in the pulsing power of organ chords swelling about us: "Praise God from whom all blessings flow." Alive in the comfort of rhythm and rhyme: "What a friend we have in Jesus." Alive in the sway and alternating footfalls of solemn processions: "Joyful, joyful, we adore you, God of glory, Lord of Love."

When I left Hollywood First Presbyterian, because of my adolescent distress at the church's aggressive anti-Communist campaign, which struck a discordant note with lessons on forgiving our enemies we were taught in Sunday School, I left Jesus behind. Not God, for God has haunted and hunted me down all my life. But Jesus. For years I didn't realize it, so closely linked in mind and experience were the divine and human that I couldn't distinguish them. But he was gone. He has emerged again, more as cipher and mystery this time than as uncomplicated, felt presence, in the form of a visual symbol: the Sacred Heart.

This book, then, is about the Sacred Heart. It is a book about the long Christian devotion to that heart—its history, iconography, prayer, theology, hymnody, and liturgical life—told against the present-day backdrop of story, poetry, visual imagery, and song. It is also a book about the way I have come to know Jesus, whose heart images our truest heart. That heart is an open, fleshy portal that invites us into the unfathomable lure of a divine love that transcends gender, image, and present experience. Finally, much to my initial surprise and certainly less obviously, this is a book about the fathers who have loved me into life.

Acknowledgments

The essays "I Thirst," "The Christ of Iglesia San Omer," and "The Vineyard of the Lord" that have been incorporated in the text first appeared, in altered form, in *Weavings* 15/4 (July/Aug. 2000); 30/5(Sept./Oct. 1998); and 16/5 (Sept./Oct. 2001). The story of Bryn Athyn is excerpted from my *The Time Between: Cycles and Rhythms in Ordinary Time* (Nashville, Tenn.: Upper Room Books, 1999), 212-220. Gratitude is due to Michael Leach and Robert Ellsberg, editors at Orbis Books, who somehow knew that this book was ready for birth. Thanks too go to Jackie Lynch of Omaha, who did the yeoman's share of word processing, and to Dean Barbara Braden of Creighton's Graduate School, who made Jackie's help possible. Fr. Joseph Power, O.S.F.S., at De Sales Resource Center was, as always, a wonderful friend and invaluable aid to research. It was Fr. Power's efforts that made a 1996 study trip to France possible and put me in conversation with other researchers interested in the Sacred Heart. The combined efforts of Fr. Power, Fr. Joseph Chorpenning, O.S.F.S., Br. Mickey McGrath, O.S.F.S., Dr. Hélene Borde, Fr. Jim Cryan, O.S.F.S., Susanne Koch, Fr. Jean-Marie Lemaire, and Sr. Grace McCormick, V.H.M., created the foundation upon which this book has been built.

The Heart's History

Sacratissimum Cor Jesu, miserere nobis!

BENZIGER & CO.   DEP. 3647   EINSIEDELN, SCHWEIZ.

Holy card
Late nineteenth century

Open to me the treasure of your most
gracious heart,
where the sum of my desires is stored.
—Gertrude the Great, 1256-c.1302

When the Sacred Heart is mentioned, most persons conjure up some memory of a polychromed plaster-of-Paris Jesus statuette, his arms outstretched or one hand pointing to the crimson, thorn-crowned heart displayed on his breast. If they are Catholic and of a certain age group, they might remember, fondly or not, obligatory family prayers around a framed portrait of a doe-eyed Christ, his person illuminated by the rays emanating from the visible crimson organ of his heart. The literally hundreds of thousands of Sacred Heart shrines, monuments, statues, prints, paintings, holy cards, medals, scapulars, jewelry, and devotional paraphernalia that litter the landscape of worldwide Catholicism reflect the fact that the Sacred Heart was one of the defining symbols of the church through the mid-twentieth century. In fact, in 1899 Pope Leo XIII formally consecrated the entire human race to the Sacred Heart. And in 1956, on the eve of Vatican II (which, ironically, signaled the diminution of religious devotions), Pius XII published *Haurietis Aquas (You Shall Draw Waters)*, the last of his doctrinal encyclicals that established the scriptural and theological foundations of the Sacred Heart devotion.

If Catholics grew up with the devotion, they will no doubt remember Thursday night adorations, First Friday observances, and novenas in preparation for the June feast. They will think of the practices of consecration and reparation, that "making up" for the neglect and abuse human beings have heaped on Jesus' heart. And they will recall the Promises of the Sacred Heart that

1

Christ purportedly communicated to St. Margaret Mary Alacoque, which include the assurance that those who receive communion on the First Friday of nine consecutive months will not die without the grace of repentance, God's mercy, and the sacraments. The first half of the twentieth century saw the publication, mainly for laity, of dozens of manuals and treatises about the Sacred Heart devotion. Although I personally find most of these overly codified, systematized, and theologized, nevertheless they are treasurehouses of modern Catholic devotional culture.[1]

But this familiar (to some) form of Sacred Heart spirituality is hardly the whole story. The germ of the formal devotion lies deep in the past. What I really have loved about messing around in a part-scholarly, part-prayerful way with the Sacred Heart over the past years is the archeological undercovering of the many layers of this image. I think it is a "primal" Christian image in the same sense that twentieth-century theologian Karl Rahner, among others, speaks of "primal words": ripe, fecund words that dwell at the core of a religious tradition and roll down over the ages, becoming richer, fuller, and more expressive. A primal image or word is not merely an illustration of scriptural texts. They have scripture at their core. But they do not stop at the boundaries of the text. Scripture is "entered" and explored through prayer, worship, and study so that the layers of meaning hidden in the literal word or image come to light. One might see these primal words and images as either gradually revealing their implicit meanings or as variously interpreted in successive cultures and moments in history. Perhaps both things are true.

The point is that the image of the Heart of God has for the length and breadth of Christianity's existence been present in some form, either incipiently or overtly. Whether as scriptural allusion, as a verbal image crafted in prayer, poetry, or song, as a theological affirmation, or as a visual image, the Heart of God has rolled down the ages, pouring out its inexhaustible content, exhibiting myriad faces, titles, and names. Becoming a prism with which the long life of the Western Christian world might be viewed. Becoming a fleshy window through which we might glimpse something of divine mystery and through which the divine mystery might gaze upon us.

The "history" of the Heart in the Western church up to Vatican II might be briefly summarized in the following way.[2] In later chapters of this book I will continue to flesh out this spare chronology.

First there was the body of Jesus, the carpenter from Nazareth. His body was hung rudely on a cross. When he died, when the body was laid in the grave, his friends' long quest for an answer began: Where is the body?, they asked.[3] Some said they saw him. The body was present again but only briefly. Soon he was gone, but he left with his friends an animating Spirit. Now they, as a community, would become his body. The mystical body of the church.

But still they looked to his cross-hung human body. They told the story. They wrote it down. They came to see that body as God's own body, as both human and divine. And they entered performatively into his body through eating and drinking.

Those in the first centuries who were later called the Fathers saw the divine-human and church bodies as mirror images of each other.[4] The story told of his body being pierced and of blood and water flowing like fountains from it. Just so, they said, the graces found in the sacraments—the waters of baptism and the blood of the eucharist—flowed like fountains from the church. As Eve was born from the side of Adam, the Fathers mused allegorically, so the church was born from the opened side of Jesus. It was, to use a spatial metaphor, as if these Fathers gazed upon the body from outside and found there a redemptive, theological answer to the body question. But then, this is no surprise. For God's body was, in these centuries, a focus of theological speculation.

It was only after a thousand years that the interiority of the body was fully explored.[5] His medieval friends became more familiar with him as a human person. They reenacted his birth by setting up a manger and putting a mewling, puking baby in it. They wondered what he thought about things. They began to wonder what he experienced, especially when he hung there on the cross. They pictured with vividness the crown of thorns, the blood, the long and torturous walk to the hill where he would be nailed and die. And they imagined the wounds. The punctured feet. The torn hands. The pierced side. Especially the side.

Ineluctably drawn, these medievals crowded about the wounded body with its opened side. And they ventured within. True devotion to the human Jesus and to his heart had begun. Elite friends cloistered in monastic cells received spousal visions of him revealing his heart. To them he opened himself, poured out his heart's secrets, invited them inside, and exchanged his heart for theirs. Others, outside cloister walls, drew rough or polished images of his heart. They showed it dangling from the cross beams, suffering, and dying of love. They knew the embodied heart as pouring itself out. On the cross. Into the hearts of friends. In the eucharistic sacrifice on the altar.

Inside his wounded, open body his friends were intimate with both the virtues of his human heart and the inexpressible love at the heart of his divinity. They were inside the very body of God. They sought to cultivate his heart's virtues, and to let him live in them.

At last, in the early modern era, the church as a body would formally honor his heart in public liturgy.[6] They would set aside a communal festal day to honor the heart, write songs, choreograph ritual practices, and articulate a theory of the divine-human heart. Although as a community the church continued to dwell inside the heart, allowing the imagery of the long communal gazing to permeate its subjective life, the devotion that the church promulgated also encouraged a "standing outside," a patron-client relationship with the heart that was primarily petitionary and intercessory.

By the eve of Vatican II, the Sacred Heart had become the virtually defining symbol of Roman Catholicism. It had been the standard under which a persecuted church rode out the terrors of the French revolution as well as the standard flown over the late-nineteenth-century church in its reactionary battle against the modern world. It was the cherished symbol that graced the walls of Irish-American immigrants and the ubiquitous image of Latin American popular devotion. Then came Vatican II with its shift of focus away from devotions to the common prayer of the liturgy and toward scripture. The ground out of which the devotion grew ebbed away.

On the contemporary American landscape the Sacred Heart appears to many as an archeological relic, a shard still visible from an antique civilization long passed away. Like an intriguing shard, I pick up the remnants of the Sacred Heart devotion, brush them off, turn them over, and try to reassemble them like the numinous puzzle they are.

Fountain of Life

"Rivers of Living Water"
Br. Michael McGrath, O.S.F.S.

It was Preparation Day, and to prevent the bodies remaining on the cross during the sabbath—since that sabbath day was a day of special solemnity—the Jews asked Pilate to have the legs broken and the bodies taken away. Consequently, the soldiers came and broke the legs of the first man who had been crucified with him and then of the other. When they came to Jesus, they found he was already dead, and so instead of breaking his legs one of the soldiers pierced his side with a lance; and immediately there came out blood and water. This is the evidence of one who saw it—trustworthy evidence, and he knows he speaks the truth—and he gives it so that you may believe as well. Because all this happened to fulfill the words of scripture:

Not one bone of his will be broken, and again, in another place scripture says: They will look on the one whom they have pierced.

—John 19:31-37, gospel reading for the
Feast of the Sacred Heart, Cycle B,
Jerusalem Bible

Fountain of Life

Out from the wound of God's body
the life-giving fountain flows forth.
We are the children of freshening streams
that pour out upon the whole earth.

Breathed into life by God's Spirit
in the womb of our mother, the Church,
we are the daughters and sons of great love:
the marriage of heaven and earth.

Born in the rush of the waters
delivered in baptismal birth,
we are the sons and the daughters of love:
heaven renewing the earth.

Free flowing fountain of mercy,
current on which justice rides.
We are the children cleansed in these streams,
carried by love's swelling tides.[7]

The intuition lies deep in the tradition: the very nature of divinity is ec-static. It pours itself out, overflowing all boundaries, propelled by its own fierce fullness. I associate the intuition most clearly with Dionysius the Pseudo-Areopagite, that sixth-century Syrian monk whose treatises *Celestial Hierar-chy* and *Mystical Theology* had such an influence on medieval thinkers and hence, through them, the later theological and spiritual tradition. Dionysius thought about the divine-human drama in terms of emanation and re-emanation. The unity that is the divine life he saw as spilling out of itself (emanation) into the multiplicity of created things in an ecstatic movement. These myriad things, because they are of the same divine stuff, if to a more diluted degree, have within them the same ecstatic drive. They are propelled to return (re-ema-nate) back to the source from which they came. Thus the cosmos, and human beings within it, express and participate in divinity's own ecstatic life: fullness that brims over, desire that explodes its own boundaries.

When the church Fathers of the first Christian centuries considered the testimony of the scriptures, they envisioned the church as born from the side of Christ. As Eve, Adam's wife, emerged from her husband's side, so the church emerged from the side of Christ. The church-bride was the issue of the bridegroom's heart. Theologians like Origen, Augustine, Ambrose, Cyprian, and Jerome linked together scripture passages and formed an ongoing inter-pretation that imaged the course of salvation as flowing from the cleft in the rock, the opened body of the crucified. In *Letters*, St. Cyprian wrote:

If men thirst, says Isaias, then God will give them water in the desert. He will make it spring for them from the rock, or the rock will be split and water will flow and my people shall drink. This was fulfilled in the Gospel when Christ, who is the true rock, was split by the thrust of the lance in his painful death. Alluding to the prediction of the prophet, he cried: If any man thirst, let him come, and let him drink who believes in me. As the Scripture says: Streams of living water shall issue from his body.[8]

The history of the heart begins with this intuition of ecstasy. That pierced side gushing with blood and water became in the minds of the church fathers a fountain. Divine life flowing forth to cleanse and to slake humankind's thirst.

The fathers "read" the crucified body of Jesus as an allegory for the body of the church; they "read" the blood and water that flowed from his pierced side as representing the sacraments of baptism and eucharist. They saw God's body as a flowing fountain of life from which salvation flowed. All who approached and drank there would receive eternal life. The Fathers proclaimed this mystery in treatises, hymns, and litanic prayers. In the fourth century Ambrose wrote:

> Drink of Christ, for he is the rock from which the
>   water springs.
> Drink of Christ, for he is the fountain of life.
> Drink of Christ, for he is the stream whose torrent
>   brought joy to the city of God.
> Drink of Christ, for he is Peace.
> Drink of Christ, for streams of living water flow
>   from his body.[9]

The medieval heart tradition continued this allegorical imagining but gave it a further Dionysian dynamism. The water and blood gushed forth from the innermost regions of divinity as self-gift, as ecstatic donation. The corpus was given visual artistic form as a fountain of life. Medieval artists showed Christ as the centerpiece of a public fountain, watering the women and men who frolicked in the free-flowing waters. The wounded body became a press from which wine was poured. Representations of a bloodied Jesus bent under the weight of his cross were drawn. From his torn flesh poured a ruddy stream which collected in a great wooden vat. Christ the Vine. Christ the Winepress. Christ the Wine.

Thus the heart's history began with this intimation: divine life is ecstatic. It flows out of itself with irresistible impetuosity. It is liquid and tumultuous. Our dryness is answered by its healing rains. Our thirst met with cooling draughts.

"I thirst." Two small words. As unobtrusive as a plain, brown-wrapped package left unopened in a storeroom. Too small, too unremarkable to open.

They are remembered as two of the last words spoken—quietly it might be supposed—just before the end. Before the giving over. Remembered, no doubt, because they are among the last recorded, and we have a penchant—all religious peoples do—for scrutinizing last utterances. Viewing them as summation arguments offered before a fence-setting jury. They clarify for us the motives, the clear trajectory of the plot that emerges from the contradictory, random evidence of a lifetime. Or we scrutinize them as we might the hieroglyphics embossed on a Mezo-American stele, exotic ciphers waiting to be decoded. Intimations of another world. Markings become rafts to carry us across the fog-shrouded mystery of another time, in this case, the as-yet-unexplored future that will some day claim us all.

They are remembered as among the last few words that Jesus uttered. Thus, they become key to knowing him. We take them, therefore, not simply as a bare statement of physiological fact: an indication that the body, tortured and deprived of the water so necessary to continue functioning, was entering its last stages of dissolution. We hear those brief words as infinitely fuller, charged with meaning.

They become the gateway through which we pass to understand who he is and who we are.

We have had virtually no fall or winter this year. Midway through December, the time of year usually giving notices of school closings or icy road conditions, the radio announcers began a common litany: "Another mild day." "Highs in the 50s." "We're all hoping for a white Christmas." "Sorry folks, no sign of flurries yet." They began to apologize for the seasonal tunes originally scheduled to reflect the winter experience: "'Let It Snow," "Sleighride," "Winter Wonderland."

They did remark, however, that the unseasonably pleasant weather made going to the malls easier: "Only ten more shopping days! Get out and buy!" I heed their advice, urged by the Christmas wish list my teenaged son presented to me, this year not tacked to the refrigerator door but professionally displayed on the computer screen as a Power Point demonstration replete with moving icons and sound.

At the intersection of 72nd and Dodge, after dropping a dollar into the Season's Greetings bucket of one of Omaha's firefighters who roam between the lines of vehicles waiting to turn at the intersection, I pull into the vast asphalt expanse that surrounds the sprawling mall complex and queue up behind a black sports utility vehicle in the conga-line of cars snaking through the lot. We dance distractedly together for a quarter of an hour until, one by one, we fall by the wayside, grateful to bring our idling motors to a halt in our earnestly sought-after stalls.

The mall is decorated for Christmas. A mammoth gold wreath with fifty-foot wire mesh bows hangs above the main entrance. Inside, hundreds of shoppers mill and graze at the festooned counters set out between permanent shops. Each tiered cart bulges with beribboned goods: overflowing baskets of processed cheese food and sausages, mechanical dogs that bark and quiver to the turn of a key, silver tins containing foot-massage oils, boxer shorts embroidered with the smiling faces of Santa and Mrs. Claus, a miniature ceramic New England village, hemp soap and shoelaces, baseball caps with the logos of American teams written in Japanese, pocket-sized electronic day planners, alpaca fleece mucklucks, scaly plastic alligators and boa constrictors, foot-high porcelain dolls costumed like characters out of *Gone with the Wind*, an ersatz crystal ball that when turned upside down predicts financial gain and romantic adventure in a husky foreign-sounding woman's voice, incense in ten aromatherapeutic scents, painted wooden music boxes that tinkle the strains of "Silent Night" and "Take Me Out to the Ballgame," sterling silver personalized tooth picks, life-sized plush pandas to which are pinned packets of bamboo seeds, a wall clock in the shape of a partially eaten apple.

The mall food court is packed with shoppers sagging under the weight of plastic bags heavy with purchases. Silver garlands loop overhead, swinging perilously between neon logos. *Amigos, Little King, China Express, Orange Julius*: lighted apparitions in a tinseled sky. In the food court's center an electronically equipped grand piano peals out the chorus of "Angels We Have Heard on High": "Glo-o-o-o-o-or-i-ah! In-ex-chel-sis-day-oh." The wafting odors of meatballs and wontons mingle with the cologne sample scents still lingering on my wrists. The mall has become a seasonal palace of sensory overload.

I make my way through the cluttered gray metallic aisles of the electronics store, find what I need, and escape as soon as I can. As I home in on the mall exit, something catches my eye. In a doorway display of an import shop is a rustic, hand-crafted crèche scene from the Caribbean nation of Haiti. The rude hut is fashioned from a half coconut shell. In front of the hut, primitive clay figurines painted in bold colors create a family scene: mother in blue, father in red, infant lying on a slab of unpainted clay, two animals, the larger brown and presumably bovine, the smaller white and goat-like, two sets of twinned onlookers, their painted barrel-bodies joined at the hip, one set crowned by gold bands with serrated edges. I stop. The swirling, sensory stimulation of the mall recedes. I realize: I thirst.

Long before Jesus said those words, or before the author of the gospel of John recorded him as saying those words, they resided in the religious consciousness of his people. Those small words sound in the psalms of anguish, in the prayers of distress poured out to God. Especially they sound in the twenty-second psalm—that song that is sung again from the ambos, pulpits, and choir lofts of Christendom each year on Good Friday—and in its sister psalms.

> My throat is dried up like baked clay,
>> My tongue cleaves to my jaws;
>> to the dust of death you have brought me down.
>>> (Ps 22:16, New American Bible)

> I looked for sympathy, but there was none;
>> for comforters, and I found none.
> Rather they put gall in my food,
>> and in my thirst, they gave me vinegar to drink.
>>> (Ps 69:21-22, New American Bible)

The thirst sung here is a sign of extremity, a plea whispered by a being crippled with pain, surrounded by hostile forces, confronted by death.

This desperate thirst that the Hebrew bible inscribes and that Jesus echoes in his last hour is primal. For thirst is perhaps the most powerful human longing, certainly more urgent than hunger. Rivaled only by the need to draw breath.

His people understood that thirst is an accurate metaphor for our need for God. Thus they sang that thirsting not only as a cry of anguish in distress. They and generations of Christians after them sang the song of thirsting as a daily prayer, a prayer that, like breath, composed the substance of life itself.

> O God, you are my God whom I seek;
>> for you my flesh pines and my soul thirsts
>> like the earth, parched, lifeless and without water.
>>> (Ps 63:2, New American Bible)

We have had virtually no fall or winter this year. Thus as I gaze out of the retreat house windows onto the prairie landscape, I see the spider-like outlines of leafless trees, a familiar winter sighting, uncharacteristically silhouetted against an eggshell blue sky and cradled in a meadow of yellow-green stubble more likely to be seen in the dry heat of a late August afternoon. It is nine days before Christmas. I have escaped from the merciless inevitability of final exams week at the University, carving a Monday and Tuesday out of a week book-ended by shopping and holiday feasting and the relentless semester-end grading to be followed swiftly by the arrival of relatives.

I have escaped: from the e-mails, voice-mails, priority mails, snail mails, overnight mails, conference calls, evaluations, assessments, applications, forms, standards, procedures, processes, requisitions, recommendations, memos, meetings, quizzes, questionnaires, colloquia, conferences, symposiums, and from the departmental, divisional, college-wide, university-wide, weekly, monthly, annual, biannual, millennial, parochial, diocesan, conference-wide, session, board, governing, advisory, consultative events. I have come parched. Thirsting for God.

Nothing here. No program. No agenda. No necessity. Only the silence of the yellow-green prairie. Only the methodical hoarding of a gray squirrel darting up and down the scaly trunk of the cottonwood. Only the dry flutter of the pages of the old bible as I turn them one by one.

> I am wearied with calling,
>   my throat is parched.
>   (Ps 69:4, New American Bible)

In the semi-circular chapel, set against a bank of windows that frame the prairie outside, is a Christmas crèche. Carved blond wood figurines perhaps ten inches high sit upon several low raised platforms draped in advent rose and purple. Two pink poinsettias. A circling of four candles. A three-sided suggestion of a stable. A kneeling mother. A father, staff in hand, on bent knee. An empty cradle. Three sheep settled for a rest. One donkey. One ox. Three barefoot shepherds, one blowing on what seems to be a primitive bag-pipe.

At the far door of the chapel, at the spot in a church where one might find the baptismal font, atop a pedestal, is a ceramic bowl filled with smooth stones. From the base of the bowl a stream of water wells up and spills out over the stones. The music of the water's flowing is the only sound in the chapel.

It is not coincidence that when the church fathers of the second, third, and fourth centuries read the passion narrative in the gospel of John, they fixed upon the piercing of his side, upon the flow of blood and water that issued there. They said (and perhaps John before them intimated) that from Christ's mystical body, as from his physical body, blood and water flowed. They said that God, the one for whom we so hunger, for whom we so thirst, came and continues to come to us as food and as fountain.

The last pale rays of sun light the leafless lace silhouetted from behind. Through the swath of cobalt blue that the upper sky has become, a phalanx of geese passes, heading south to avoid the late arriving winter. Their faint honking falls farther and farther away.

As in those midlife dimmings that sometimes happen, it has become more and more difficult to slake my thirst for God in the particular manifestations of church in which I find myself. Preaching rings hollow. Music, once the substance of prayer, becomes a battleground for conflicting liturgical tastes. Love takes the form of regulations beyond which one may not venture. Community grows cold. Issues divide us: church polity, doctrine, worship, biblical interpretations, homosexuality, abortion, divorce and remarriage, reproductive technology, the death penalty, school prayer, the exercise of authority, ordination, family values. Parish councils divide, sessions divide, bishops divide, laypeople divide, conferences divide, congregations divide. Building renovations divided us all. Church growth is the synonym for lived faith.

I have been too long in the ranks of those whose profession is religion, those without the freedom simply to sit in the pew and let the wonder of it wash over them. I have been too long responsible for it, accountable to it, one of those to whom people come for answers and advice.

I wish it were simply a question of shifting parishes, or denominations, a question of seeking out a more intentional small faith community, a question of experimenting with new ways to pray. It is none of these. The center does not hold. Nothing holds. In this mild, deceptive December, it is winter in my soul. I thirst.

> As the deer pants for streams of water,
>   so my soul pants for you, O God.
> My soul thirsts for God,
>   for the living God.
>   (Ps 42:1-2, English Bible)

Well before dawn I rise and enter the darkened chapel. On the north wall, a reminder of the Roman Catholic origins of the ecumenical center, is a gold tabernacle in which the sacrament is reserved. A flickering votive candle marks the presence. I settle myself on a nest of pillows gathered near the tabernacle and wait.

In the solemn dark neither the spider-like limbs of trees outside nor the advent crèche scene inside are yet visible. The unseen cradle remains empty, a place hollowed out where God's thirst for us and our thirst for God might meet. It is quiet. The ceramic stone fountain has been left unplugged during the night. Only a faint honking, a reminder that the geese phalanx is continuing south, breaks the deep silence. Only that and the sound of my soul panting at the edge of the stream.

Wash.
  Yes—
    cleanse,
flood, rinse,
    scour,
    soak,
    bathe
    me
    in that pool,
    pond,
    fountain,
    ocean,
    of your life.

On the Breast of God

John, the Beloved Disciple
on the Breast of Jesus
Fourteenth-century wood sculpture

Belong totally to God. Think of him and he will think of you. He has drawn you to himself so that you may be his; he will take care of you. Do not be afraid, for if little chicks feel perfectly safe when they are under their mother's wings, how secure should the children of God feel under his paternal protection! So be at peace, since you are one of these children; and let your weary, listless heart rest against the sacred, loving breast of this Savior who, by his providence is a father to his children, and by his gentle, tender love is a mother to them.
   —St. Francis de Sales, 1567-1622

It was Origen. Brilliant Alexandrian. Self-mutilated eunuch. Antique troubadour who sang of the martyrs as second Christs. He whose audacious theologizing whipped a generation of desert ascetics into frenzied argumentation. It was Origen (c. 185- c. 254) who in the early third century gave us John, the archetype of contemplative wisdom.

In one simple exegetical leap. No leap, really, for an Alexandrian habituated to allegorical reading of the scripture. Just a modest step. An analogical meander from the Johannine gospel's version of the Last Supper to the Platonic ideals of the contemplative life. "Now there was leaning on Jesus' bosom one of his disciples, whom Jesus loved" (John 13:23), the King James version quaintly puts it. And Origen in his *Commentary on the Song of Songs* comments, "This signifies that John rested in Jesus' innermost heart and in the inner meanings of his teachings."[10]

The intimate proximity was important. And the location. It imaged for Origen the stance of the lover of wisdom. Close to the divine secrets. Intimate with eternal gnosis. Nestled on the breast. Close to the heart.

This intuition, that nestled next to the heart on the breast of the divine-human body one may find wisdom, has permeated the heart tradition and profoundly shaped the later devotional practices associated with it. Not only did objective salvation flow from the wounded side. There was also a contemplative, even mystical, knowing to be had in that same region. John was the one who learned there. He was the beloved disciple. Hence, generations of men and women who aspired to discipleship through the contemplative path claimed John as archetype and companion to their way.

From Christianity's earliest days there has been a contemplative path, the way of those for whom salvation did not stop at the baptismal font but for whom sacramental participation was merely the gateway into a transformed seeing and, ultimately, a transformed life. Desert abbas and ammas, solitaries and monastery dwellers, recluses, anchorites and hermits, contemplative prayers of every ilk and generation have sought to participate in the radically transfiguring energy of the Christ event through intimate participation. Generations have sought the recovery of the *imago dei*, the true self grounded in divine life that is exposed when the false, ego-constructed self is gradually peeled away. This contemplative path is often conceptualized in the tradition as a resting near the divine-human heart. Correspondingly, it is a path that is carried out in a disciple's own heart.

The words of contemporary interpreter and practitioner William Shannon express this truth well.

> We see reality differently. We experience our true self and experience that self in God. We are aware that we are nothing apart from God. This is what the early Christian writers called the discovery of the heart: the heart not as a physical organ, but as the center of our being, the place where we are most truly ourselves, the place where we experience God, the place where we find our sisters and brothers in an entirely new way.[11]

I love it that fourteen centuries after Origen exigeted the thirteenth chapter of the gospel of John at the catechetical school in Alexandria, Egypt, Margaret Mary Alacoque, a young Visitation nun in an obscure convent in the provincial French village of Paray-le-Monial received in a vision the appellation "beloved disciple of the Sacred Heart." It was on December 29, 1692, the feast of St. John, and Margaret Mary, a cloistered contemplative, was praying before the blessed sacrament when she felt herself penetrated by the divine presence which, prompting her to "repose for a long time upon the Sacred Breast," then proceeded to disclose to her the "secrets of His Sacred Heart."[12]

I love it too that modern Protestant hymnals usually contain "Near to the Heart of God," the favored hymn written in 1901 by Missouri Christian Cleland Boyd McAfee after two of his young nieces died from diphtheria. Although the hymn's referent is less the transformed seeing of the contemplative life than the final hoped for rest, nevertheless the hymnic imagery of the heart speaks exquisitely of beloved intimacy with the divine.

> There is a place of quiet rest,
> Near to the Heart of God,
> A place where sin cannot molest
> Near to the Heart of God.
> O Jesus, blest Redeemer,
> Sent from the Heart of God,
> Hold us, who wait before thee,
> Near to the Heart of God.

> They sit in an uneasy circle around the room.
>   One widowed,
>   one broken from divorce,
>   the others in various stages
>   of psychic rupture.
>   Retreating from the church,
>   from laws that are
>   odd mazes
>   and they rats
>   scurrying through passages
>   forever finding new dead ends,
>
>   from principles that fit their lives
>   less well than clothes
>   handed down by a well-meaning
>   acquaintance
>   folded in a brown sack.
>
> I invite them to enter into the divine embrace.
>   We have no time for such things, they
>   complain.
>   We are active people, not recluses.

But when they weep late into the night,
when they shuffle their sorrow
back and forth
in hearts made raw from pain,
they long to hide their faces in that soft crook
of flesh between her arm and breast
and feel the heartbeat of God.

The Cleft in the Rock

Heart of Jesus Surrounded by Wounds
Fifteenth-century German woodcut
and manuscript illumination

At the time when I first began to receive these favors—I think it was during the first or second year, in the winter—I found in a book a short prayer with these words:

> *Lord Jesus Christ, Son of the Living God, grant that I may, with all my heart, all my desire, and with a thirsting soul, aspire toward you; and in you, most sweet and pleasant, take my rest. With my whole spirit and all that is within me,*

may I sigh always for you in whom alone is true blessedness to be found. Inscribe with your precious blood, most merciful Lord, your wounds on my heart that I may read in them both your suffering and your love. May the memory of your wounds ever remain in the secret places of my heart, to stir up within me your compassionate sorrow, so that the flame of your love may be enkindled in me. Grant also that all creatures may become vile to me, and that you may become the only sweetness of my heart.

I was so pleased with this little prayer that I repeated it often with great fervor; and you, who never refuse to grant the requests of the humble, were to grant me the effects of this prayer.[13]

—Gertrude of Helfta, 1256-c. 1302

Wounds

Marcus Borg says they have to be there.
The marks.

Because if
when he rose
the flesh were clean,

18

It would mean
   he had merely passed through.
   Not borne the true weight
   of love.

They have to be there.
Like a woman's body
   bears the marks
   of childbirth.

Marcus Borg didn't say that.
   I do.

A primal image, like the heart, is not static in either its visual or its poetic form. The church Fathers laid the groundwork, oriented the community toward the region of the heart, as it were. But spiritual allegory gradually gave way to something else, especially in the Western church. The body became not only a wondrous sign of cosmic or salvific significance. It became not only an image of the church-bride born from the pierced side out of which flowed sacramental streams. It was not only a code for the contemplative life. It was a living body in which a heart beat.

In the years we know as the high medieval era—in the eleventh and twelfth and especially the thirteenth centuries—Christian spirituality in the West began to focus on the humanity of Jesus. This reflected the fundamental orientation of Western culture toward the concrete, particular, human, and moral dimensions of life. His life story began to matter. Not just his resurrection but his incarnation and passion arose in the devotional consciousness of the Christian community. Intense imitation and participation in the life, passion, and death of Jesus became the sine qua non of the Christian life.

This is when true devotion to the heart itself can be said first to have arisen. The medieval praying community (for this was soon a practice of all types of people, not simply of the spiritual elite) entered more deeply into the body of Christ. Allegory gave way to an intensely personal piety that focused not only on the man Jesus—his birth, life, and death—but on his bodily wounds. The side wound especially became the object of devotion.

Medieval litanies, prayers, accounts of visions and treatises that had the wounds as their focal point abounded. Among my favorites is a long-forgotten prayer by an anonymous twelfth-century writer. For centuries it was attributed to Bernard of Clairvaux (1090-1153).

Who, beholding the disposition of Christ's body, is not transported to hope and confident petition? See, his head is bent to kiss, his arms are outstretched to embrace, his hands are pierced to give, his side is open to love, his feet are nailed to stay with us, his body has become pliable to be given to us.[14]

Visual images of the wounds began to appear. Often they were shown with the implements of the passion. The spear, the dice, the crown of thorns were drawn, in stylized fashion, along with the pierced hands and feet. The almond-shaped side wound was also depicted. Sometimes the cross was there. Not often with a realistic corpus—that would come later—but studded with the cruel implements of crucifixion and the wounds that they caused. Devotion to the wounds of Christ was associated first with the great religious orders of the Middle Ages: Cistercians, Benedictines, Franciscans, Dominicans, and Carthusians. It eventually spread to the laity, and with the upsurge in popular religiosity that began in the thirteenth and expanded rapidly in the following centuries, the wounds became a familiar devotional image.

The opened side was still the gateway through which salvation poured. It was the aperture through which the new life gestated in the womb of God was birthed. But it was also a portal through which one could enter. The side wound was the entryway to God's most secret life. It was, devotionally speaking, only a short step inward from the side wound to the heart. That organ was to become the supreme symbol of the loving intimacy between creator and creatures. Medieval Christians moved deeper and deeper into the body through the side wound into the divine-human heart where the mystery of a love that poured itself out in death could be explored.

Medieval Christian spirituality was affective, participatory, and somatic. Experience was key. To know God was to feel what God-with-us felt, especially when agonizing on the cross. To know God was to participate in the drama of Jesus' life. Thus that quintessential medieval, Francis of Assisi, acted out in literal ways the theater of the naked infant become a poor man who dies abandoned on a cross. Thus devout laypeople, adherents of the fourteenth-century "Modern Devotion," meditated daily and in turn on the pain of the five wounds of Christ. Thus medieval mystics who desired union sought intimacy inside the refuge of the wound. They plunged deeper into the divine life and entered its core, the heart. Thus Bernard of Clairvaux in his rhapsodic prose on the Song of Songs could pray:

But as for me, whatever is lacking in my own resources I appropriate for myself from the Heart of the Lord, which overflows with mercy. And there is no lack of clefts by which they are poured out. . . . "The iron pierced his soul" and his Heart has drawn near so that he is no longer one who cannot sympathize with my weakness. The secret of his Heart is laid open through the clefts of his body; that mighty mystery of love is

laid open, laid open too the tender mercies of our God, in which the
morning sun from on high has risen upon us.[15]

Bernard's lavish devotional language makes us aware of the process by which
so much of the medieval heart tradition developed. The imagery of the "cleft
in the rock" is an allusion to the Song of Songs: "O my dove in the clefts of
the rock, in the secret recesses of the cliff, let me see you, let me hear your
voice" (2:14, New American Bible). Bernard had preached eloquently and in
detail to his monastic brethren of the Song of Songs as an allegory of the love
shared by the contemplative soul and God. And the last poignant phrase of
his prayer, "laid open too the tender mercies of our God, in which the morning sun from on high has risen upon us," echoes the ancient Canticle of
Zechariah found in the infancy narratives of Luke's gospel. The canticle proph-
esies the dawning light of the incarnation, the birth of salvation. This canticle
is traditionally the closing hymn of the liturgy for morning prayer.

Bernard, as a follower of the Rule of St. Benedict (the Cistercians were a
twelfth-century Benedictine reform), was chiefly and continually engaged in
the celebration of the liturgical hours of the church, which included morning
prayer. Scriptural passages and allusions in this context were not studied as
academic subjects but were gradually internalized through the medium of
repetitive sung prayer. In such a lifelong meditative process, threads of words,
phrases, and texts interweave with personal and communal experience. Thus
the wounded side becomes the cleft in the rock into which the contemplative
beloved is invited. And through the cleft streams the morning sun of divine
mercy. The birth, death, and rising are subsumed in imagery both visual and
poetic. The languages of erotic love, mystical union, cosmic redemption, scriptural record, and spiritual insight converge.

> Enter, O my soul, enter into the right side of thy crucified Lord. Enter
> through this blessed wound into the centre of the all-loving Heart of
> Jesus, pierced through for love of thee. Take thy rest in the clefts of the
> Rock sheltered from the tempests of the world. Enter into thy God!
> Covered with herbage and fragrant flowers, the path of life lies open
> before thee. This is the way of salvation, the bridge leading to heaven.[16]

His muscular brown torso is bent in a mirror-image S. A spiral of tensile
agony. Heavy black beard pressed painfully into a raised right clavicle. The
wounds are visible—red-stained apertures pierce belly, upraised hands, and
the one front-flung foot. But there is no cross. No tree from which this hanged
man dangles. The Christ of the Church of San Omer de Santiago de los

Cabarellos in the Dominican Republic hovers above me, a mortally wounded bird, wings outstretched in free flight, drawn upward not with the strength of limbs, not with the force of chin thrust forward. But with head sunk, limbs crumpled, propelled by the burning of some hidden inner fire.

From the courtyard encircling San Omer, the construction workers' metallic hammering punctuates the low babble of the gathered *campesinos*. They rock, lounge, walk, wait at the end of a pilgrimage of hot-bussed days. They have come in hundreds. An army of Bartimaeuses. Come for healing of *los ojos*, the eyes. Patched. Poked. Peered into. Soothed. Swabbed. Sutured. They have been met at the end of the pilgrimage route by *doctores Americanos* fresh from the land of the free, of the brave. Come with opthamological instruments, with surgical beds, with privileged expertise to restore sight.

A *campesina* enters the breezeway that separates the courtyard from the wide, red-tiled sanctuary of the church. Her walk up the center aisle between erratic rows of straw-seated, straight-backed chairs is sure. She kneels at her destination—the low step fronting the white-laced altar and the cylindrical gold tabernacle. Her mute gesture is as profound as it is inarticulate. She wears a white-dotted, navy-blue shirtwaist.

Another comes, twenty years older, wearing a gray sweatshirt over brown cotton trousers. A third sports a mottled green blouse tucked into a full, swinging skirt of coordinating color. She is perhaps forty, but her gesture is the same. Not a polite, socially expected genuflection at the communion rail. Not the emotive crouching of the lost-who-have-been-found at an altar call. Hers is a gesture of deep dignity. Of simple humility. The rightful, silent yielding to the magnitude of the mystery at the core of all that is.

The white-dotted, gray, and mottled-green *campesinas* return down the aisle. They acknowledge, each in her own way, the muscular brown corpus in free flight on San Omer's west wall, his wings arching upward, lofted by the hidden fire.

He is not brown but white on the south wall of the *enfermería* that faces San Omer's. He looks out over a steel sea of opthamologists' pincers and tubular vials of multicolored pills. He stands upright, kindly eyes gazing solicitously over the cabinets bursting with ointments and salves. Pale robes slung over his shoulders are pulled back to reveal his breast. On it glows a shimmering emblem, a thorn-wreathed heart glowing from the heat of its own fire. A pointed finger leads my eye to the vibrant organ. His gaze invites adoration.

It is said, in the devotional tradition, that Jesus died, not of the soldier's lance, not of the suffocation caused by the weight of his dangling body. It is said he died of a broken heart. Of love so tender it tore the tissues of the earth's finest fashioning. Burst the boundaries of creation's wildest, most wonderful imagining.

On San Omer's east wall is the first of the fourteen terra cotta tablets that encircle the sanctuary—*Jesus es sentenciado a muerte* (Jesus is condemned to death). The tablets are a visual and ambulatory pilgrimage of the heart's wounds. Below that first tablet is a small metal plaque.

In memoriam our beloved son
Peter Francis de Ruyter
Dec. 29, 1990–Dec. 31, 1990

And a hand-calligraphed poem too poignant to be held in the heart more than a moment. From a woman. And a man. Whose empty arms and weeping ended one December in *Amen*. Niched there under the bowed terra cotta head of a man whose arms are bound and whose feet are set on a path that leads through sorrow to a mystery too mute for words and a pain that cracks itself open. Wounds through which the world walks. A portal wide enough for a universe of suffering to enter into the sanctuary where the rightful gesture is adoration and the fitting word *Amen*.

A fluorescent-green chameleon slithers down the wall behind San Omer's cylindrical gold tabernacle. Two *campesinas* enter at the far end of the sanctuary. One wears a rumpled, rose-colored sweater and broad, wrap-around sunglasses, a gift from the *doctores* of the brave, free land. Her companion, green plastic sandals matching the chameleon's skin, helps her to her knees. They creep the last three yards to the low step before the altar.

Outside, the hammering of the workers continues. A banana palm brushes gently against the western breezeway adjacent to the flying Christ. Mosquitoes seek their lunch in the exposed flesh of my neck.

Here in this midlife waistline of the globe, this slightly going-to-seed, ripe-to-the-point-of-rotting bioregion of the earth, the world's sorrow makes its slow, sad pilgrimage toward that great, breaking portal that opens wide enough so that all may enter and say *Amen*.

The textbook open on my lap informs me:

Paradoxically, it is among those who most intimately know the power of death, that we find the most stubborn faith in the power of life and therefore in the power of God who is the source of life. This faith in the ultimate goodness of life, even in the midst of affliction, is at the heart of Latino popular Catholicism.[17]

There is an ironic freedom in this rural Caribbean poverty. Freedom from the furtive, frenetic activity of maintaining the illusion of cultural immortality, of technical mastery of the secrets of the universe that is the birthright of the brave and free. Here, where a shared song, an *hola*, a handshake, and a dazzling smile form the infrastructure of culture in place of electricity and sanitation, there is freedom from the pretense of self-sufficiency. The primal skeletal structures of human life—birth and death, feasting and fasting, mourning and rejoicing—are laid bare here. Here too is exposed the primal mystery of the gaping wound burst open in the heart of God.

In the *baño* behind the sacristy of San Omer's, Arturo swabs the red-tiled floors with a long-handled mop. Three nights ago in the circular shade of the bandstand, to the pulsing rhythms of Latin CDs, Arturo taught us to merengue and to bachata. And, assuring us that it was well beyond the capacity of cool-blooded *Norte Americanos*, entertained us with a flamboyant solo performance of the salsa. Then, flashing his dazzling smile and deliciously unaware of his unveiled machismo, Arturo instructed his male American students to lead, to lead. Like driving a car, he insisted, firmly maneuvering his flushed and giggling American partner backward as he whirled and swayed and displayed the magnificent plumage of his muscled masculinity. Arturo. A celebration of the simple fact of existence.

When the mystery of the Godhead spoke itself to the world that had emerged from its own ripe, generative belly, it spoke in the language of the heart. It spoke a tenderness so poignant it would break our hearts if only we would be still enough. If only we would cross those last few yards on our knees. It is said, in the devotional tradition, that when the body of God was broken open so we could peer inside to divinity's inmost depths, it was discovered that the heart itself was pierced. Not by the soldier's lance, for that entered the body's right side. Instead, the heart, lodged in the chest's left cavity, was pierced by Love's own longing.

The electric lights in the neighborhood surrounding San Omer periodically shut off during the evening and nighttime hours each day. There simply is not enough to go around. Electricity. Gas. Health care. Funds for roads. For sanitation. Education. Housing. There is simply not enough. In the great handsome barn of a supermarket near San Omer, in whose parking lot from a cantilevered lookout nest a car-guard surveys the assembled automobiles, they sell handsomely packaged products from the land of the brave and free, the freshness dates of whose contents have expired. Stale pretzels. Rancid oil. Graham crackers dust-dry and soft between the teeth. Checkout clerks wear the once-fashionable castoffs that float down ocean currents from the north.

Here in this waistline of the globe, the wounds of the world fester and go untreated. Their symptoms patched and swabbed perhaps by the genuinely well-meaning *doctores*. But their causes go untouched. Legions of conquistadors, neighboring conquerors, native military dictatorships, self-interested foreign strategic defense operations have trod over this island paradise and cut wounds deep and oozing into its soil.

But the muscular brown man in free flight on the west wall of San Omer's is not pinned. Not nailed down. His wounds, though bloody, do not fester. They are a fountain, a swift-running river. He flies free. Propelled by some hidden inner fire.

White-visaged on the wall of the *enfermería* he seeks us out with kindly eyes and points to the luminous thorn-crowned organ that smolders on his breast, a furnace in which to cauterize the wounds of the world.

The Heart's Bride

"Thou hast wounded my heart, my sister, my spouse" (Song of Songs 4:9)
Thirteenth-century illuminated manuscript

You have ravished my heart, my sister, my bride,
you have ravished my heart with one glance of your eyes,
with one bead of your necklace.
How beautiful is your love, my sister, my bride,
how much more delightful is your love than wine,
and the fragrance of your ointments than all spices!
—Song of Songs 4:9-10,
New American Bible

The lush devotional imagery that flowed from St. Bernard's prayers was not atypical of medieval heart spirituality. Prayers, hymns, and treatises issuing from medieval convents were saturated in bridal symbolism. The cloistered nun understood her vocation in nuptial terms. She was a bride of Christ. Monastic males also framed their spiritual itineraries in bridal metaphors. Images from the Song of Songs, that hymn that celebrates the dance of lovers, became a template for understanding the soul's search for divine intimacy. Here the language of the heart flourished.

Imagery from the heart tradition was also inextricably woven into the warp and woof of theological reflection. Take, for example, Bonaventure (c. 1217-74), the towering theologian of the Franciscan tradition. His extended meditation on the humanity and passion of Christ, *The Tree of Life*, explores in sensate detail the drama of salvation and redemption played out on the world stage. By then ancient themes from the tradition of the heart—saving fountain, the dove in the cleft, the pierced side—resonate in his reflection on the fruits of the cross, the tree of life.

> Behold how the spear thrown . . . through the divine mercy fastened in the wall without making a wound and made a cleft in the rock and a hollow place in the cliff as an abode for doves.

Rise, therefore, beloved of Christ,
> be like the dove that makes its nest in the heights
>> in the mouth of a cleft.

There,
> like a sparrow that finds a home,
> do not cease to keep watch:

there,
> like the turtledove,
> hide the offsprings of your chaste love;

there
> apply your mouth
> to draw water from the Savior's fountains

for this is the river arising from the midst of paradise
which, divided into four branches and flowing into devout hearts, waters and makes fertile the whole earth.[18]

I love Bonaventure. I love too the female medieval mystics of the tradition of love mysticism. They are numerous. I think first of the cluster of spiritual luminaries from the thirteenth century. Some were cloistered members or associates of the German Benedictine-Cistercian monastery of Helfta: Gertrude the Great of Helfta, Mechthild of Hackeborn, Gertrude of Hackeborn, Mechthild of Magdeburg.[19] Others, like Hadewijch of Brabant, were part of the loosely knit communities of beguines, holy women who led lives of apostolic poverty and prayer without monastic vows. Still others—Beatrice of Nazareth is an example—were from other monastic communities. They, and other females whose spiritual writings or life stories have been preserved, like playful lovers frolicked in the fields of prayer. Jesus was their joy. Love was their song. The mystical marriage their goal and joy. Heart imagery laced through their meditations like an intoxicating liquor.

Here is Gertrude of Helfta (1251-1302)—Gertrude the Great—whose extraordinary experiences of the heart of Christ went well beyond ruminative poetry or prayerful theological reflection. The heart burst forth from Gertrude's inner life in visions and locutions. In *Herald of Divine Love* she recorded the course of her growing intimacy with God. A vehement impulse to intimacy drove her prayer. Often, she prayed of and from the heart.

I was so pleased with this little prayer that I repeated it often with greater fervor; and you, who never refuse to grant the requests of the humble, were to grant me the effects of the prayer.[20]

The effects were in fact dramatic.

After I had received the life-giving sacrament, on returning to my place, it seemed to me as if, on the right side of the Crucified painted in the book, that is to say, on the wound in the side, a ray of sunlight with a sharp point like an arrow came forth and spread itself out for a moment and drew back. Then it spread out again. It continued like this for a while and affected me gently but deeply. But even so my desire was not fully satisfied until the Wednesday when, after Mass, the faithful venerate the mystery of your adorable Incarnation and Annunciation. I too tried to apply myself to this devotion, but less worthily. Suddenly you appeared, inflicting a wound in my heart, and saying: "May all the affections of your heart be concentrated here: all pleasure, hope, joy, sorrow, fear, and the rest; may they all be fixed in my love."[21]

Gertrude did not experience these divine favors in isolation but was nurtured within a community that encouraged a devotional life that bled easily into visionary experience.

At once it occurred to me that I had heard it said that wounds have to be bathed, anointed, and bandaged. You had not then taught me how to do this, but afterward you showed me through another person. She was more accustomed, I believe, to listen more frequently and consistently, for the sake of your glory, to the soft murmur of your love than was I, alas. She now advised me to meditate devoutly on the love of your heart as you hung on the cross, so that from the fountains of charity flowing from the fervor of such inexpressible love I might draw the waters of devotion that wash away all offenses; and from the fluid of tenderness exuded by the sweetness of such inestimable love, I might derive the ointment of gratitude, balm against all adversity; and in efficacious charity perfected by the strength of such incomprehensible love, I might derive the bandage of holiness, so that all my thoughts, words, and deeds, in the strength of your love, might be turned toward you and thus cleave indissolubly to you.[22]

The monastic compatriot referred to here was Mechthild of Hackeborn, a recipient of equally wonderful spiritual graces. This account allows a glimpse into the symbiotic and mutual spiritual guidance these medieval women of the Helfta community enjoyed. The narrator recounts Gertrude's visit to Mechthild, her sister in religion.

When she reflected on her wretched and worthless state, she thought she was quite unworthy of such great gifts as those with which she knew God was constantly enriching her. She went to Dame Mechthild of happy memory, who was held in great esteem and honor for her grace of revelations. She humbly begged her to ask the Lord about the gifts mentioned above, not because she was in any doubt or wanted to be reassured, but because she wanted to arouse in herself a greater sense of gratitude and to be confirmed in faith, lest afterward she be led to doubt by her sense of her extreme unworthiness. Dame Mechthild, as she had been asked, took counsel with the Lord in prayer. She saw the Lord Jesus as a Spouse, full of grace and vigor, fairer than a thousand angels. He was clad in green garments that seemed to be lined with gold. And she for whom she had prayed was being tenderly enfolded by his right arm, so that her left side, where the heart is, was held close to the opening of the wound of love; she for her part was seen to be enfolding him in the embrace of her left arm. Full of wonderment, blessed Mechthild desired to know what the meaning of this vision might be. The Lord said to her: "Know that the green color of my garments lined with gold signifies that my divine works are ever green and flourishing with love." And he continued: "Everything in this soul is green and flourishing. And this close proximity of her heart to the wound in my side means that I have so joined her heart to mine that she is able to receive, directly and at all times, the flow of my divinity."[23]

For these medieval female mystics the heart was a nuptial chamber, an intimate environment into which they, wise virgins, were invited to commune with their beloved. Their imagery was frankly erotic, but it would be a mistake for us in the twenty-first century—citizens of the most eroticized of cultures and heirs to Freudian assumptions that all forms of love are traceable to the libido—to interpret these medieval ecstasies through a reductive lens.[24] Instead, the primal image of the heart at this medieval moment served as a visionary spatial metaphor of the breathtaking intimacy of divine and human life.

Seven Sweet Songs

You led me here.
No.
My love for you led me.

Here.
To this bare room
so that I might
give myself to you.

At the threshold,
soldiers
catch the soft fabrics
that ease from shoulders,
waist,
thighs.

Naked I enter
and begin to sing.

                            "forgive them . . . "

A lover's crooning.

                          . . . "be with me . . . "

Circling the bed
upon which we will lie.

                          "behold . . . behold . . . "

Giving my body,
I extend my arms,
recline,
receive your embrace.

                          . . . "am I forsaken?"

My soft moaning
born of this wonderful sweetness.

                          . . . "I thirst . . . "

My heart ripens,
splits open,

                          "finished"

so you,
you,
love,
might enter
and find yourself at home.   . . . "into your hands . . . " [25]

The Table of the Heart

"The Eucharistic Banquet"
German Benedictine monastic
devotional drawing
fourteenth century

Yet it was I who taught Ephraim to walk
  who took them in my arms;
I drew them with human cords,
  with bands of love;
I fostered them like one
  who raises an infant to his cheeks;
Yet, though I stooped to feed my child,
  they did not know that I was their healer.
. . .
My heart is overwhelmed.
  My pity is stirred.
I will not give vent to my blazing anger,
  I will not destroy Ephraim again;
For I am God and not man,
  the Holy One present among you;
I will not let the flames consume you.
      —Hosea 11:3-4, 8c-9, first reading
      for the Feast of the Sacred Heart,
      Cycle B, New American Bible

Awonderful devotional drawing, produced by an anonymous German Benedictine nun at the turn of the sixteenth century, shows a heart-shaped enclosure within which a nun and two other figures are seated at a table spread with a blue and white striped cloth. One figure, a bearded young man, holds out to the nun what appears to be a loaf of bread. The second figure stands tenderly behind the nun and seems to present her to the bread-bearing young man.[26] A haloed dove perched on the table proffers a chalice clutched between its talons.

The painter, from the abbey of St. Walburg, created this image, now titled "The Eucharistic Banquet," as a visual aid for herself and her community during meditation. The drawing functioned as a mirror, prompting the meditator to "live into" the reality depicted there. On one level, what is shown is a mystical union of the contemplative pray-er with heavenly personages, an intimate sharing in the heavenly banquet that the eucharist enacts. On a somewhat less esoteric level, what is urged is a transformation of heart: the setting

31

of a eucharistic banquet in one's own heart. Devotional drawings such as this one were apparently much used in monastic communities in the fifteenth and sixteenth centuries, and they point to the intention cultivated through contemplative practice, word, image and ritual gesture, to change, to become what one is not yet.

The St. Walburg image is rustic, a folk-art creation. But its intended use is fairly sophisticated for it invites participant-viewers into its heart-shaped frame in order that they might begin to dwell in the reality that the artist depicts. Indeed, gazing at the image, even in a reproduction, I feel as though I might take just one short step over the threshold of the brown, wood-textured frame and find myself standing on the moist carpet of grass in the picture's foreground. From there it would be a natural motion to slide up a chair, seat myself at the simple cloth-spread table, and join the friendly gathering of sacred banqueters.

And I shall clothe myself in your eternal will,
and by this light I shall come to know
that you, eternal Trinity,
are table
and food
and waiter for us.[27]

—Catherine of Siena, fourteenth century

From earliest times, the church has associated the side—and thus the heart—of Christ with the sacraments of the church, especially baptism and eucharist. In the patristic era John Chrysostom (c. 347-407) wrote:

> The lance of the soldier opened the side of Christ, and behold, from his wounded side Christ built the Church, as once the first mother, Eve, was formed from Adam. Hence Paul says: Of his flesh we are and of his bone. By that he means the wounded side of Jesus. As God took the rib out of Adam's side and from it formed the woman, so Christ gives us water and blood from his wounded side and forms from it the Church . . . there the slumber of Adam, here the death-sleep of Jesus.[28]

But the reading that Chrysostom—called the Golden-Mouthed—provided was allegorical. It wasn't until the Middle Ages that the fleshy luxuriance of the symbol was so fully explored. In the thirteenth century, eucharistic theology was at the forefront of the church's thinking as Thomas Aquinas, spurred by the newly recovered philosophy of Aristotle, clarified how it was that during the consecration a change was effected in the "substance" of the bread and wine (which *become* the body and blood) while the "accidents" (the outward appearance) remained unchanged. At virtually the same time, in 1264, Pope Urban IV instituted the Feast of Corpus Christi (the Body of Christ).

Placing this feast on the church's calendar meant that Christians everywhere in the West now turned special liturgical attention to the mystery encoded in the ritual that was at once a meal, a recapitulation of the divine sacrifice, and a literal and spiritual participation in the Jesus-event, hence, in divine life itself. The mystical and devotional life of European Christendom came alive with eucharistic visions and ecstasies. The women of the medieval mystical tradition began to express their intense religious longing in eucharistic terms.

Contemporary scholars, spurred on by the insights of medieval historian Carolyn Walker Bynum, have summed up medieval women's spirituality in the phrase "holy feast, holy fast."[29] Theirs was the domain of matter, of food and bodies, both in secular and religious life. Food preparation and serving. Nursing and tending. Bodies of babies. Bodies of the sick. Bodies of the dead. Thus the great female mystics of this era also acted out their religiosity in gustatory terms. They, however, did not have primary access to the eucharistic body of Christ. The handling of the sacred elements was reserved to the male clergy. Women could only be recipients. Yet in their prayer, which some of them recorded for the edification of others, they consumed that body with gustatory relish. They miraculously survived on the eucharist alone. They clamored for frequent communion, a practice unheard of at the time.

Mostly, they saw themselves as fed and nourished by the eucharistic banquet. That feasting did not stop, however, at the cessation of the liturgy. Dining at the promised banquet, communing with God by eating and drinking, became a common motif of high medieval women's religious literature, prayers, and mystical experience. Although she is more well-known then other medieval visionaries, the following visionary account by Catherine of Siena (1347-1380) is not singular. In it the motifs of eating and drinking, suffering, eucharistic feasting, the sacred wounds, and imitation overlap. The vision occurred simultaneous with her developing inability to eat, her eucharistic craving, and her growing compulsion to serve others by suffering.

> On the night following . . . a vision [of Christ with his five wounds] was granted to her as she was at prayer. . . . "My beloved," [Christ] said to her, "you have now gone through many struggles for my sake. . . . I today shall give you a drink that transcends in perfection any that human nature can provide. . . . " With that, he tenderly placed his right hand on her neck, and drew her toward the wound in his side. "Drink, daughter, from my side," he said, "and by that draught your soul shall become enraptured with such delight that your very body, which for my

sake you have denied, shall be inundated with its overflowing goodness."
Drawn close . . . to the outlet of the Fountain of Life, she fastened her
lips upon that sacred wound, and still more eagerly the mouth of her
soul, and there she slaked her thirst.[30]

The visceral communion Catherine enjoyed, her lips pressed to the pierced
side, translates seamlessly into the prayer in which she sang the Trinity itself
as table, waiter, and food at a banquet.

> You, eternal Father,
> are the table
> that offers us as food
> the Lamb, your only-begotten Son.
> He is the most exquisite of foods for us,
> both in his teaching,
> which nourishes us in your will,
> and in the sacrament
> that we receive in holy communion,
> which feeds and strengthens us
> while we are pilgrim travelers in this life.
> And the Holy Spirit
> is indeed a waiter for us,
> for he serves us this teaching
> by enlightening our mind's eye with it
> and inspiring us to follow it.
> And he serves us charity for our neighbors
> and hunger to have as our food
> souls
> and the salvation of the whole world
> for the Father's honor.
> So we see that souls enlightened in you,
> true light, never let a moment pass
> without eating this exquisite food
> for your honor.[31]

What is it that we do when we gather at the moment of communion? Do
we memorialize the last supper Jesus held with his disciples? Do we enter
sacred time and recapitulate Jesus' sacrifice on the cross? Is this our sharing
in the eschatological banquet? Is this a reenactment in a new key of ancient
Israel's temple sacrifice? Or a refocusing of the Passover event? The place

and time we become God's mystical body? The ritualization of our mutual need and nourishment? A thanksgiving? Are we recipients? Ones who share with one another? Ones who prepare to go forth and share with others? Sacrifice ourselves for others? All or some or none of the above?

Scripture points us in (at least) two directions in our thinking about the meaning of that last supper that Jesus celebrated with his friends, the supper at which he is depicted, through ritual gesture, as linking this meal with his impending death. "This is my body, which is given up for you," he says, while taking up the bread they are all to eat. "This is my blood," he says while passing the cup.

Interestingly, the synoptic gospels and the Johannine account differ in their temporal placement of that supper held in the upper room. Matthew, Mark, and Luke portray it as an actual Passover meal, a Jewish ritual that celebrates the people's exodus from slavery in the land of Egypt and God's merciful intervention in that liberation. While the sacrifice of a lamb is depicted as part of the liberating action in Egypt and as an element of the feast itself, the supper itself is focal. John's gospel, in contrast, underscores the sacrificial symbolism of the event by placing the meeting of the disciples early in the holy season, before the Passover meal. It thus coincides with the ritual slaying of the Passover lambs, a highly significant coincidence of which John's prescient Jesus is fully aware. The early church did institute the eucharist at Passover time, and Christian writers from St. Paul onward have claimed that the death of Christ was the fulfillment of the sacrifice foreshadowed by the Passover. But sacrifice does not exhaust the meaning of this central performative ritual action.

The mid-twentieth-century church brought to the fore the symbolism of the banquet that the medieval mystics had explored. Virgil Michel, the Benedictine priest whose innovative consideration of matters of worship launched the Catholic liturgical renewal early in the twentieth century and paved the way for the cataclysm of Vatican II, saw both the liturgy and the gathered church—the body of Christ—as transformative. From our intimate interconnection with one another in the body of Christ and in the eucharistic meal, in Michel's mind, flowed our sense of interconnection with all others. At the table the poor are rich, and the rich are no more than the poorest of the poor. For the Benedictine, the ritual action of bringing oneself as gift to the worship experience, one's receptivity to the word "broken open," the offering (not simply of money and talents) of self to God and others, and then the self-offering of God, are enacted at the eucharistic table. This mutual human-divine self-giving imprints on the worshiper the paradigmatic actions that will/should be reenacted in daily life. The liturgy, for Michel, was thus a school of social transformation.

Seen in this way, liturgy is a performative celebration of our mutual need and nourishment, and of our physical and spiritual hungers, both individual and communal. Hence, it is metaphorically not only the sacrifice of a victim but the self-donation of a breast-feeding mother or the generous hospitality of the host of a festal meal. It conjures up images of the eschatological banquet toward which the compass of Christian hope points.

The memories run together like the wet wash of a child's watercolor, more tactile and visual than verbal.

1952. My small left hand is tucked in his larger and protective right as we amble together past the modest wood bungalows down the steep grade of the asphalt sidewalk. His summer-weight shirt fans open at the collar. The stiff flounce of my dotted-swiss skirt brushes rhythmically against my knees. A summer evening in my childhood Los Angeles—still slow-paced and hazy with the hint of cookouts. As is our weekly custom, my father and I have kissed mother goodbye (dodging the edge of her wide-brimmed sun hat), waved at the retreating red Renault as it carries her off to her archeology class, and headed downhill toward Happy Hollow restaurant. Soon we will be seated across from each other on the benches of the stiff, vinyl-backed booth perusing the enormous triptych of the children's menu, which offers gustatory meditations in balloon-shaped hues of red, blue, and yellow. We will discuss the evening's choices, turning them over on anticipatory tongues. No doubt, as always, the grilled cheese on white will tempt me. We are dining out, and I am very pleased.

1956. Palo Alto. We thumb through a set of photographs taken at my recent ninth birthday party: gaggles of grade school girls in pastel framed against the polka dots of flowering margueritas. I slide one photo quickly to the bottom of the pile, avoiding the image of myself, cheeks flushed, gaze lustful, leaning into the open door of the waist-high oven to greet the birthday cake as it emerges from its incubation. Caught in sunlight, the camera turns my eyes red and gold. I repress the shame the picture elicits. In the kitchen photo I wear a loose shirt and wide pants, which hide the fact that my mother shops for me in the section of the department store euphemistically labeled "Chubettes."

The 1960s. The memories speed up and run together like a fast-forwarded film. Recess in junior high: surreptitiously surrendering to the impulse to slip back into the snack line to procure just one more sticky cinnamon roll before the bell rings. The mouth-drying, rubbery, hard-boiled egg diets of my high school years. College, the struggle begins in earnest: I memorize calorie charts and religiously scrape aside any carbohydrates on a plate; faint from hunger, I watch a single red apple drop from its niche in a campus vending machine; the insipid warmth of diuretic teas; on a cool California afternoon, I huddle over the floor vent to stave off the chill that has invaded my bones; I fixate on the dismissive comment of a representative of the Civic Light Opera who has just heard my vocal audition: "Well first, you need to lose ten, fifteen, twenty pounds"; it is difficult to keep up with a Central America art history tour group, my head swims, yet I refuse to eat a proffered banana because it is on the forbidden foods list.

Later, distinct memories emerge into full focus.

December, 1975. We are less than a dozen, an intimate gathering of family and friends settled into the cushions of the handsome Georgian furniture that graces the parlor of this convent-turned-retreat-house. The woman who is my sponsor in this initiatory rite is a religious and a calligrapher. She reads the reflection I have chosen for the occasion: Ignatius of Antioch's meditation entitled "Three Hidden Mysteries Wrought in the Silence of God." We are a motley gathering: two other nuns, one the director of the retreat house; my soon to be second husband; a childhood friend who has long since abandoned her oppressive Irish Catholic upbringing to embrace Tibetan Buddhism; my Jungian analyst, daughter of Southern California's leading Hasidic rabbi.

My *doktorvater* is here in spirit—he has sent a wonderful letter—but is on sabbatical in Syracuse with his family. Still, I carry him with me, for it was he who first introduced me to this place. He who stood with me on the steps of the Old Mission after a class field trip and looked with me out over the adobe roofed city to the sparkling sliver of the Pacific on the horizon. It was he who knew my hunger. When I said, "I feel as though I belong here," it was he who had responded, "Yes, I do too." My parents are here too, proud and supportive and somewhat outside their frame of reference.

The Franciscan who presides at the coffee-table liturgy has been my confidant and faithful listener for over a year. Saturday mornings we have met in the dim anterooms of the Old Mission, adobe walls and tiled floors protecting the nighttime chill from the anticipated onslaught of the South Coast sunlight. I am here to receive communion for the first time.

1978. The steam-clouded shower stall in our modest Santa Barbara apartment. I am stealing a rare unencumbered moment in the pink-tiled sanctuary of our bathroom, letting long, hot jets of water pour over my weary flesh.

Our three-month-old daughter, visible through the bathroom door, is buttressed on the bed between two rolled flannel crib blankets, taking her nap. The warm wetness prompts my active lactation sensors and ribbons of thin, blue-white milk arch and merge into the thundering shower cascades. A few foods I now avoid—garlic and raw onions, vegetables of the cabbage family—because they produce colicky symptoms in nursing babies. But food is now a joy, a purposeful necessity, sustenance given to sustain another.

Imago Dei

Sacred Heart thank-offering
Jesuit Gardens
Creighton University,
Omaha, Nebraska

Beloved, let us love one another, because love is of God; everyone who loves is begotten by God and knows God. Whoever is without love does not know God, for God is love. In this way the love of God was revealed to us: God sent his only Son into the world so that we might have life through him. In this is love: not that we have loved God, but that he loved us and sent his Son as expiation of our sins. Beloved, if God so loved us, we also must love one another. No one has ever seen God. Yet, if we love one another, God remains in us, and his love is brought to perfection in us.

This is how we know that we remain in him and he in us, that he has given us of his Spirit. Moreover, we have seen and testify that the Father sent his Son as savior of the world. Whoever acknowledges that Jesus is the Son of God, God remains in him and he in God. We have come to know and to believe in the love God has for us.

God is love, and whoever remains in love remains in God and God in him.

—1 John 4:7-16, second reading
for the Feast of the Sacred Heart,
Cycle A, New American Bible

Sometimes I wander through the Jesuit gardens tucked away behind the administration building on the university campus where I teach. Although the present-day Jesuit community has stamped the garden with the contemporary style of its red brick and glass residence, the environment's older heritage is still evident in the form of an abandoned, white-washed brick planetarium (the brainchild of one of the early Jesuits of the astronomy faculty), in a rock-tiled grotto from which in summer a thin rivulet of water flows from the vine-covered feet of a plaster statue of Mary, and in the life-sized figure of Christ, his gentle head bowed slightly, left arm extended forward in a gesture of welcome, and right hand pointed to a flame-tipped heart visible just above the drape of his robes. On the pedestal that enthrones him an inscription reads:

> THANK-OFFERING
> OF THE STUDENTS
> FOR PROTECTION
> IN THE
> WORLD-WIDE PLAGUE
> OF THE WAR YEAR
> 1918

The plague referred to, of course, is the virulent influenza epidemic of 1918, which killed upward of twenty-five million people worldwide. I am aware of the referent because this was the epidemic in which my grandmother, Ruby, my father's mother, died. The year 1918 saw the end of the "war to end all wars," the U.S. Senate vote on women's suffrage, and the saga of the Bolsheviks in Russia. It was the year that my father, aged seven, lost his mother and received the wound that, in his eighty-four years, never quite healed.

What a strange and compelling thought! That God might take bodily form and that, by approaching, touching, and then entering that body, we might become intimate with, might *know* God. The literalness both compels and repels. After all, a literal reading of scripture can lead to the narrow cul-de-sac of fundamentalism. And the thought that the infinite mystery we call God might be adequately expressed as anything so fragile and finite as a human being is, on the surface of it, silly. But there it is, again and again in the spiritual tradition: the marveling, the astonishment
    —that infinity became cloistered in a dear womb
    —that the Lord of the universe reclined for the sake of the universe.
    —that God on the fruit-laden tree bowed down for our hunger.
    —that God's self revelation was as a helpless child.

And there is that other equally although not quite so incomprehensibly strange insight: that the tender particularity of finite life allows access to that which transcends and far outstretches finitude. This, at least, makes more sense. The sacramental sensibility of the Catholic Christian tradition makes itself tangibly felt here in the intuition that the creation, fashioned as it is by a divine creator, bears the impress of the hands that made it. It is felt even more accurately in the intuition that human beings are *imago dei*, made in the image and likeness of God. Thus, a deep and careful knowing of humanity can yield some true knowledge of God. The same fundamental danger is here as well. Just as one might claim that God's immensity has been once and for all captured in one specific translation of a revealed text (only *these* words, said *this* way!), one might also claim that we can with certainty (by utilizing our own genius and perhaps with a little more time) accurately analyze and account for the divine/created universe.

But if the dual insights are allowed to be open-ended, if they do not restrict but instead acknowledge that vast remnant of our experience that defies expression, then they are powerful insights that excite the mind, heart, and imagination.

There is something in God and something in us that correspond. We come from, have our being in, and return to God. In the tradition of the heart, that correspondence is love. Love, not merely as sentiment or feeling, but love as the inner dynamism of God in God's triune self. Love as the generative power that overcomes death. Love as self-donation. Love as the welcome of the "other" as another self. Love as the gravitational force that binds all disparate things together. Love as the fire that burns clean and as the balm that heals. Love as the vision that sees the integrity of both parts and whole. Love as source and end and the path between.

The tradition of the heart does not say merely that God loves us "because," or that God's love can be seen "in," but that God *is* Love. And that God's very essence truly in some small way might be encountered here and now.

Mary's Question

Small, dear heart
   nested under mine:
how is it
   you are great enough
   to encompass all
    and everything?

Imagining the Heart

Drawing displayed at the novitiate at Paray-le-Monial, France, 1685, during Margaret Mary Alacoque's tenure as novice mistress

He opened the gate of his Heart, the treasure house of the blessed God-head, and she entered as into a vineyard. There she saw from dawn to dusk a river of living water, and around the river twelve trees carrying twelve fruits which are the virtues St. Paul speaks of in his Epistle: love, joy, peace and so forth.

—Mechthild of Hackeborn,
thirteenth century

The Sacred Heart is such a Catholic thing. During the Reformation much of Christendom, especially those who followed what became known as the Magisterial Reform, shied away from the vivid and fleshy devotional imagery that had flourished in the heart tradition. Not that the reformers were all iconoclasts. The zealous wing— Zwingli, Karlstat, and later Calvin— was. But many Protestant reformers used imagery, especially printed engravings and woodcuts, to great advantage. Nonetheless, their images became more biblically grounded, less grotesquely imaginative, and more illustrative of moral and theological teachings than the imagery that flourished before the reforms.[32] In this context visual renderings of the heart as a separate cultic object receded.

The Roman Catholic Church also concerned itself with the reform of religious imagery. Here the heart image was continued, even elevated. But official prescriptions regulating the production and use of images flourished in the centuries after the Reformation. The official iconography of the Sacred Heart did not emerge until the end of the seventeenth century. Two principal forms predominated. The first was the free-standing heart anticipated by the pen-and-ink created to Visitation nun Margaret Mary Alacoque's visionary specifications. The image Margaret Mary saw in her great revelations, and which in 1685 she instructed a novice to replicate, was Jesus' heart, inscribed with the word *caritas*, pierced by nails, surmounted by a cross wrapped in flames and encircled with a crown of thorns. The names of the extended Holy Family—Jesus, Mary, Joseph, Joachim, and Anne—surround the image. The second image—the one that eventually was used for public display—had the heart displayed exteriorly on the breast of Christ. The preferred theological message was visually underlined: It is Jesus Christ who is the proper object of worship. The 1878 and 1891 directives from the Congregation of Rites in Rome required that all images displayed for public veneration had to show the heart embedded on the divine breast (not free-standing or in the hand) and that images of the heart alone be permitted only in private devotion. Thus, we get the beginning of the visualization of the Sacred Heart with which most people are familiar: Jesus with the flowing robes, his heart displayed prominently on his breast.

An admission. This particular visual manifestation of the heart doesn't do it for me. Perhaps I should rephrase it more generously. The aesthetic of most popular nineteenth- and twentieth-century devotional images of the Sacred Heart does not communicate to me the power inherent in the symbol. It's too sentimental. I know that it has fueled the imaginations of generations of pious Catholics. I know as well that the regulation of religious imagery serves an important theological purpose: some grotesque pre-reform heart images encourage morbid fascination more than worship, and some created during the romantic era—lacy holy cards with ornate hearts raining down "mystical dew" from heaven, heart shaped porcelain holy water fonts into whose rosebud-encircled side wound one dips one's finger—can degenerate into trivializing kitsch.[33] I know too that the theology of the Sacred Heart that evolved from the seventeenth through the early twentieth century has excited and sustained many good souls. That theology doesn't do it for me either. I take comfort in the fact that in this I am not alone. I felt immense relief when I first discovered that Teilhard de Chardin, the early-twentieth-century theologian and paleontologist, felt that way too.

> Everybody knows the historical background of the cult of the Sacred Heart (or the love of Christ): how it was always latent in the church, and then in the France of Louis XIV assumed an astounding vigorous form which was at the same time oddly limited both in the object to which it was directed ("Reparation") and in its symbol (the heart of our Savior, depicted with cautiously anatomical realism!).
>
> The remains of this narrow view can still, unfortunately be seen today. . . . I was not yet in "theology" when, through and under the symbol of the "Sacred Heart," the Divine had already taken on for me the form, the consistence, and the properties of an ENERGY, of a FIRE.[34]

Teilhard is right about the constriction of the cult as it developed after the seventeenth century. Earlier, often rough-hewn images of the heart speak more provocatively to me. Especially the free-standing, thorn-encircled hearts or the hearts pinioned helplessly to a cross. All the deliciously bizarre images that my earnest, theologically updated religious women colleagues have struggled so hard since Vatican II to reimagine, reinterpret, or frankly move beyond.

The rustic images can be stimuli for the imagination. In fact, that is the intended use of much of medieval devotional religious imagery. Images were in part didactic—the old saw about stained-glass windows inserted in cathedrals for the illiterate peasantry—but they were also self-consciously formative. They encouraged a pray-er to enter through the material image into the imagination, where worlds are made and possibilities glimpsed.

The imagination has unfortunately been given short shrift in Western thought. Clearly, this is an oversimplification, but for the most part both the biblical record and subsequent philosophy and theology have tended to characterize the imagination simply as the human ability to make images and to see it as opposed to the human faculty—whether reason or nonconceptual thought—that can allow us true access to the divine.

We have lingered long with a fear of idolatry ("Thou shalt have no other gods before me") and hence of images we perceive to be of our own fashioning. We have seen ourselves, as we position ourselves in close proximity to grave scriptural admonitions, as setting up idols fashioned in our own limiting images. And this is not an insignificant concern! The history of humankind *is* littered with the debris of our stubborn insistence on deifying ourselves: our cultures, our languages, our racial and ethnic inheritances.

We have, however, also assumed that our very capacity to create images, visual and verbal, both inside our heads and outside with our hands, is therefore suspect. Or more benignly, we equate the imagination with fantasy, with optional amusement that bears little on the serious issues of life. We see imagination as that rare creative capacity belonging solely to the artists among us.

Here is Augustine (354-430) speaking at the waning moment of the ancient world about his own religious conversion.

> For my mind ranged in imagination over shapes and forms that are familiar to the eye, and I did not realize that the power of thought, by which I formed these images, was something quite different from them. ... I withdrew my thoughts from their normal course and drew back from the confusion of images which pressed upon it so that it might discover what light it was that had been shed upon it when it proclaimed for certain that what was immutable was better than that which was not. ... Then, at last, I caught sight of your invisible nature.[35]

And here is Blaise Pascal (1623-1662), at the dawn of the modern era, philosophizing:

> Imagination. It is the dominant faculty in man, master of error and false-hood, all the more deceptive for not being invariably so. . . .
>
> This arrogant force, which checks and documents its enemy, reason, for the pleasure of showing of the power it has in every sphere, has established a second nature in man. . . . It deadens the senses, it arouses them; it has its fools and sages. . . .
>
> This deceptive faculty [is] apparently given to us for the specific purpose of leading us into error.[36]

On the whole, theology (I'm oversimplifying again) has discredited the power of the imagination. Yet ironically, when Augustine relaxed from the exertion of recounting for us his conversion to that which is immaterial and thus beyond imagining, he turned to his rhetorician's bag of tricks and waxed luxurious in metaphors that attempted to communicate something of that ancient-yet-ever-new beauty that he intuited is at the core of all things. Metaphoric language, of course, being one of the chief linguistic expressions of the imagination!

As contemporary Anglican theologian Paul Avis, among others, points out, the primal Christian message is cast in metaphor, symbol, and mythic form (*myth* not meaning "fictional" but referring to the cacophony of imaginative images that profoundly shape our conceptions of the divine and provide spiritual and moral blueprints for human life).[37] Avis, following thinkers like Suzanne Langer and Paul Ricoeur, takes images and the imagination seriously.

My favorite theorist, a man steeped in literary theory, is William F. Lynch (1908-1987), a mid-twentieth-century Jesuit scholar who both studied literature and drama and engaged in theological reflection.[38] For Lynch, faith itself was a type of imaginative activity. He argued, against the dominant Scholastic theology of his day, that faith was not best understood as the acceptance of propositional truths on the authority of another, whether this was based on a credible reasoning or not. Lynch drew on thinkers like Newman and some Catholic modernists rather than the dominant neo-Scholastics. He also drew deeply from the wellsprings of his own religious experience. He was a Jesuit, thus he was steeped in the methodology of Ignatius of Loyola's practices of prayer. Ignatius began with the finite world. It is through this finite world, he believed (in Christian humanist fashion), that the infinite is approached. Not by bypassing the finite, sort of leap-frogging over it in an act of spiritual aspiration. Not in ignoring or denying concrete reality in favor of an idealized vision of the "really real." Ignatius, and Lynch following him, sensed that the deepest dimension of the finite is its ability to communicate the infinite. Within the very *structure* of the finite there exists, unconfusedly yet inseparably, the infinite. There is simply no other entryway to God than through the created world.

Lynch rejected the overarching "integratist" theology of his day, which viewed truth as having fallen from heaven "in a convenient system of logically interlocked univocal propositions."[39] Instead, true knowledge for him was dialectical, analogous, and personal. Knowledge was an activity performed by a person, lived in relation to this changing world; knowledge generated perspectives that are analogous to former ways of knowing but never simply the same.

This is where the imagination comes in. Lynch posited that humanity's basic tool for achieving reliable knowledge is the analogical imagination. The imagination is our image-making capacity, but it is not a separate faculty in opposition to other faculties. Instead, it is

> not a single or special faculty. It is all the resources of man, all his faculties, his whole history, his whole life, and his whole heritage, all brought to bear upon the concrete world inside and outside of himself, to form images of the world, and thus to find it, cope with it, shape it, even make it. The task of the imagination is to imagine the real. However, that might also very well mean making the real, making the world, for every image formed by everybody is an active step, for good or for bad.[40]

Lynch alerts us: imagination, and hence images, matter!

The prelude occurred in a Los Angeles public library. A modest local branch. At one of those long, polished, blond, wood tables arranged at appropriate intervals between the stacks so that patrons might have a surface upon which to work. It was the late sixties, and my young husband and I were seated across from each other at the narrow table. He was buried in the theater script for a Hollywood playhouse production for which he hoped to audition. I had come along for the ride. Our conversation of the previous evening was on my mind. I, the non-Catholic who had nevertheless signed on the dotted line and agreed to have our future children raised in the church, was baffled by his lack of interest in his middle name.

"Why were you given it?"

"I don't know."

"Are you named for somebody?"

"St. Hubert, I think."

"Who was St. Hubert?"

"I don't know."

So when I stumbled across a faded nineteenth-century volume entitled *Lives of the Saints* tucked on one of the shelves just above our table, it was natural I should want to research Hubert and find out what made him a saint.

Perhaps I should mention that I was studying history at the time, having returned to school in my mid twenties after a stint as a performer—in and out of the Hollywood unemployment office between jobs. I liked finding out about the deep history of my present-day existence. Living on the far western lip of the North American continent sheltered by palm trees and fanned by the Pacific's salt-sea winds, I nevertheless sensed that my story reached way back beyond my post–World War II birth. My family history could be traced backward across the tall grass prairies of the Canadian prairie, beyond the rough colonial settlements of early America, across the turbulent expanses of the Atlantic, and into the fortressed stone structures of medieval and early modern Europe and the British Isles. My patrimony was the languages, the legal and economic systems, the symbols and gestures embedded in Western European culture. That included religion.

So I set out to find out about Hubert. It turned out that he was an early Christian bishop, a scholar of sorts, and I read with interest about his home life, education, travels, and his negotiations with foreign dignitaries. I was chugging along just fine until I came to a description of Hubert's ability to bilocate. The historical narrative melded seamlessly into a matter-of-fact statement about Hubert's simultaneous appearance in North Africa and continental Europe. This was followed by a nonchalant prose passage detailing the saint's many miraculous exploits. Profoundly disoriented, I closed the book. In fact, I felt queasy. It was as though two subterranean tectonic plates had collided inside the structured universe in which I lived.

In retrospect, I know this was one moment of many at the time that brought about my inexorable turning toward God and the Catholic faith. This was my introduction to a layered universe, to a conceptual world in which time and space ceased to have the boundaries that my empirically trained mind assumed. Here was a world suffused with a power that did not conform to necessity. Here was a world drenched with grace.

Interestingly, at the time I did not assume that what I had read of Hubert's paranormal exploits was simply superstition or the mumbo jumbo of long-ago illiterate minds. Since that time I have learned to understand the literary genre of hagiography and can now discourse interpretatively across these varied conceptual worlds for my students and colleagues. But then, the shock of the colliding worlds of historically verifiable fact and dreamed-for possibility was traumatic.

A layered reality is part of the Catholic imagination. To possess this imagination is to dwell in a universe inhabited by unseen presences—the presence of God, the presence of the saints, the presence of one another. There are no isolated individuals but rather unique beings whose deepest life is discovered in and through one another. This life transcends the confines of space and time.

While Jesus is a historical figure and might function in our lives as an exemplar and model and his death and resurrection as a salvific event that affects the future, still the Catholic imagination wants to push the boundaries of life beyond this. We—and Jesus and the saints—exist in some essential way outside the chronology of historical time. We have being beyond the strictures of geographical space. And we can sense this now, in the concreteness of our lives.

The tradition of the heart makes this vividly, even grotesquely, clear. The divine-human correspondence is intimate. It is discovered in the flesh. Our fleshy hearts are fitted for all that is beyond flesh by conforming to the heart of Jesus. That divine-human heart is the passageway between earth and heaven. That heart is the tactile tracings of divine love on the created order. That heart is the widest, wildest longing of humankind's own love.

The Virtues of the Heart

Hope does not disappoint, because the love of God has been poured out into our hearts through the Holy Spirit that has been given to us. For Christ, while we were still helpless, yet died at the appointed time for the ungodly. Indeed, only with difficulty does one die for a just person, though perhaps for a good person one might even find courage to die. But God proves his love for us in that while we were still sinners Christ died for us. How much more then, since we are now justified by his blood, will we be saved through him from the wrath. Indeed, if, while we were enemies, we were reconciled to God through the death of his Son, how much more, once reconciled will we be saved by his life. Not only that, but we also boast of God through our Lord Jesus Christ, through whom we have now received reconciliation.

The Child Jesus Sweeping Out
the Human Heart
Engraving
Wierex Brothers, seventeenth century

—Romans 5:5-11, second reading
for the Feast of the Sacred Heart,
Cycle C, New American Bible

Gentlest of Hearts

Gentlest of hearts, become our heart.
Seamless our ending and our start.
Knit us so tightly with gentle strength
Our lives become one width, one length.

Sweetest of hearts, become our song
Poured out in melodies simple and strong.
Words as truth's trumpet, deeds justly drummed
Compassion the strings of the lives that we strum.

Tenderest of hearts, become our nest,
Sought-after shelter, place of our rest.
Fold us in mercy, cradle in care,
Held in the arms of the love you prepare.

Warmest of hearts, become our fire
Fueling the embers of love's desire.
Love as the cautery, love as the balm
Healing the wounded world all our lives long.

Most gracious of hearts become our way.
Delight in our labor, joy in our play.
Dawn brings your hopefulness, nightfall your faith,
Love is our daily fare, nurtured by grace.

Gentlest of hearts, become our peace.
Our vengeance disarm, our hatreds cease.
Forgiving ourselves, we set others free,
Children of God as you mean us to be.[41]

The one contribution that the English language makes to the Christian theological vocabulary, I am told, is the word *atonement*. Segment it into its component parts, and its etymological meaning is laid bare: at-one-ment. Being one with. This is the Christian life. God becoming one with humankind. Humans becoming one with God. The "one-ing" is written for us in and on the flesh of Jesus.

This is the deep grammar of the heart tradition. This one-ing. Julian of Norwich in the fourteenth century, echoing Psalm 103, called it "kinship" and cast God's mercy in the language of "kindness." God becomes our kind. We become kin to God.

In one way or another the heart tradition has always meant this. It always presumed, implied, a radical participation. But the way that participation is to take place has been variously understood. For the church Fathers, it was first and foremost an objective participation that took place through the sacramental life of the church. Those streams of living water flowing from the pierced side were baptismal. The medieval era, without abandoning the objective one-ing—in fact, sacramental theory was given formal definition at this time—did lean into the subjective experience of becoming one in its extravagant devotionalism and its florid visionary tradition. Hence the mystical patterning that produced the dramatic exchange of Jesus' and Catherine of Siena's hearts, Gertrude the Great's visions of Christ revealing his heart, and

Lutgard of Aywiere's prayer experiences of nursing at the open wound in the Savior's breast.

The early modern period, in its turn, gave us most clearly a sense of what it would mean to participate not only in redemption or in the mystical marriage but in the character of Christ. The early modern age delineates for us the virtues of the heart. Not that Christian consideration of the virtues was new at this point. From the ancient sayings of the desert ammas and abbas we derive an articulate language of vices and virtues—the famous seven deadly sins are an offshoot of this. The vices are to struggle against. The virtues will be infused, graciously given. But early modern Europe, turning from the extravagant devotionalism and theatrical spirituality of the Middle Ages, emphasized the formation of virtuous character as central to the Christian life.

For centuries the sevenfold list had been assumed. There were faith, hope, and charity, the three theological virtues (so named because they have a scriptural basis—Paul delineates them). Then there were the four "cardinal virtues" deduced from ancient Greco-Roman thought: justice, prudence, fortitude, and mercy. This septagonal template provided perimeters for Christian reflection on the virtues. But it did not exhaust the possible list.

However they were conceptualized, it was the formation of Christian character that the early modern world emphasized. To "live Jesus" was to cultivate as one's own the qualities of Christ's heart.

"Come to me, all you who labor and are overburdened, and I will give you rest. Shoulder my yoke and learn from me, for I am gentle and humble in heart, and you will find rest for your souls. Yes, my yoke is easy and my burden light."
—Mt 11:28, gospel reading
for the Feast of the Sacred Heart,
Cycle A, Jerusalem Bible

It really is Francis de Sales (1567-1622) who gifts the heart tradition with the idea that the heart of Christ is gentle and humble. I have a theory that in the course of undergoing the *Spiritual Exercises* of St. Ignatius as a young man (Francis was schooled by Jesuits at the College of Clermont in Paris), the future saint was "met" by the Jesus of Matthew 11—the Jesus who invites all of us, the weary and overburdened, to come to him.

When you "do" the *Exercises*, a spiritually disciplined and transformative process engaged in with an experienced guide, you are invited to enter imaginatively into the archetypal Christian drama of creation, fall, and redemption. Along the way you come to realize in a deeply personal and individual way that you have been infinitely loved, and you are invited to align yourself with that Love. Classically, the "exercise" you engage in as you choose that alignment is done imaginatively by envisioning yourself on a battlefield between two encampments. One represents all that is dominated by that which thwarts and resists Love. This is Satan's army. Another represents all that champions goodness and Love. This is the army gathered under the standard of Christ. You are supposed to enter into the drama of the scene with all five senses and choose Christ's standard as the one under which you will encamp.

This "Meditation on the Two Standards" is just part of a much more involved meditative process that invites the "exercitant" into an intimate communion and identity with the Christ who ushers in God's reign on earth. Along the way the fabric of the exercitant's own life story becomes interwoven with the Christ story. The exercitant's distinctive prayer experiences supply texture and individual character to the archetypal narrative.

Francis de Sales, as I surmise, may well have seized upon the image of Jesus revealed in Matthew 11: "Come to me, and learn from me, for I am gentle and humble of heart." This single, simple insight informs the entire Salesian spiritual tradition that Francis, along with his spiritual friend Jane de Chantal, founded. At the core of that tradition is the affirmation that every human person—cleric or lay person, woman or man, married or celibate—is called to holiness. In *Introduction to the Devout Life* Francis outlined spiritual practices for lay people adapted to the contours of lives that were not at all monastic. But he wrote and preached as well for Visitation nuns—a community that he and Jane de Chantal co-founded. Indeed, as a reforming bishop in the militant Roman church that emerged in the wake of the Protestant challenge, Francis was convinced that God was raising up devout people in all walks of life to act as leaven in the loaf of a rising, revitalized Catholic Christian community.

In all of this the heart was central. In fact, the entire edifice of the Salesian spiritual vision is undergirded by the image of the heart. Reading through the voluminous writings produced by the founding Salesian saints, one is struck with the fact that on virtually every page there is some reference to "heart" or use of affective language associated with the heart. This is not the external, formalized devotion to the Sacred Heart that later came into being but a vision of an "interconnected world of hearts"—the hearts of God and humankind bridged by the crucified heart of Jesus.[42]

For Francis and Jane, the heart was the core of a person. It was not merely the seat of emotion but the seat of the intellect and the will. If one wished to persuade or encourage, one must "win the heart." For Francis, preaching (and he was a great preacher) was the art of speaking "heart to heart." For Jane, spiritual direction within a religious community was a matter of "winning hearts."

This Salesian emphasis on reaching the hearts of others was not sentimentality but rather was grounded in a rich theological vision. At its center was the affirmation of a God of love. Using compelling metaphors, Francis pointed at divine Love by describing God as a beating, breathing heart out of which the created world flows and back to which creation is drawn. Humankind, created in the divine image and likeness, participates in divine life precisely through this indrawing (inspiration) and outflowing (aspiration) movement of heart. Union with God, the end of all created being, is thus a union of hearts: a reciprocal divine-human love relationship, a mutual breathing and beating of hearts. This is Love's creative intention.

But because of sin, human hearts do not always beat in rhythm with divine love. The innate human capacity and the divine desire is there (hence the fabled "optimism" of Salesian spirituality), but hearts must be reshaped and renewed for Love's full realization. What is needed is a heart both divine and human that can, as it were, synchronize the arrhythmic movements of the human heart. This is the crucified heart of Jesus.

The heart of the Crucified is, in the Salesian vision, both a model and a reality that, through formative practice, comes to indwell in each heart. "I no longer live, but Christ lives in me," St. Paul's dictum, is transformed in Salesian spirituality into the affirmation *"Vive Jesus!"*: "Live Jesus!"

The Jesus called upon to live in human hearts is the gentle, humble Jesus of Matthew 11. Both Jane and Francis spoke at length of the "little virtues," those unspectacular, highly relational virtues like humility, patience, simplicity, cordiality, and gentleness—especially and particularly gentleness.[43] To cultivate these little virtues was to practice the lessons of the heart of Jesus. Such practice was attainable in every circumstance and station in life. It was not, however, a merely sentimental practice but a practice based on a vigorous, even eschatologically vivifying, sense of the human mandate. If all hearts were to surrender to the heart of the crucified Lord—let Jesus live—the result would be not only radically transformed individuals but a radically transformed world. To state it in a different idiom, the kingdom would come.

The Salesian world of hearts was not merely a vertical one—the hearts of individuals linked to the divine heart by the heart of Jesus—but a horizontal one as well. The breathing and beating of a human heart afire with the love of God communicated itself to other hearts and set them likewise aflame. Love's fire was ignited not through force or fear but through gentle persuasion, encouragement, and the mutual exercise of giving and receiving love.

Salesian spirituality was thus profoundly relational. All the exercises of human interaction in the service of a transformed world were emphasized: preaching, spiritual direction, charitable service, and distinctively and pointedly, the exercise of spiritual friendship.[44] Each interaction was to proceed from a heart gentled and transformed by and into the heart of Jesus.

The congregation of the Visitation of Holy Mary that Jane and Francis co-founded was the issue of their remarkable friendship. Its name recalls the mystery found in the Lucan infancy narratives—the visitation of Mary to her cousin Elizabeth. These two women, to outward eyes engaged in the most ordinary of life's tasks, yet carrying within themselves the astonishing and cosmic drama of salvation. They meet, and in that humble heart-to-heart meeting joy leaps up and the magnificent drama of God's saving love is proclaimed.

The Visitation was established as a community for women drawn to profound love of God but who, because of frail health, disabilities, or family circumstances (including widowhood), were not suitable candidates for the austere reformed religious orders of the day. Visitandines were to create a tiny world of hearts where love reigned and gentleness and humility were cultivated. In 1611, the year following the congregation's beginning, Francis wrote to Jane of an inspired thought which had come to him during the night:

> Our house of the Visitation is, by His grace, noble and important enough to have is own coat of arms, . . . So I have thought, dear Mother, if you agree, we should take as our coat of arms a single heart pierced by two arrows, the whole enclosed in a crown of thorns, and with the poor heart serving to hold and support a cross which surmounts it; and the heart is to be engraved with the sacred names of Jesus and Mary. Dear daughter, the next time we meet I shall tell you a great many little thoughts which I had on this subject; for indeed our little congregation is the work of the hearts of Jesus and Mary. Our dying Saviour gave birth to us by the wound in His Sacred Heart; it is therefore perfectly right that by constant mortification our own heart should always remain surrounded by the crown of thorns which once rested on our Master's head while love held Him pinned to the throne of His mortal sufferings.[45]

These nighttime thoughts were later fashioned into visual form and became the distinguishing insignia of the Visitation order, that each woman wore engraved on her silver pectoral cross.

The Salesian universe was an imaginative vision grounded in scripture and tradition which envisioned a world of interconnected hearts: the hearts of God and humankind united in the divine-human heart of Jesus.

"Come to me and learn from me
    for I am gentle and humble of heart."

The flight from Los Angeles to Omaha, with a layover in St. Louis, was a long one. It gave me ample time to absorb the events of the previous two days.[46] I had retraced my itinerary of twenty-three years before, following the same highway I had traveled when I left the City of Angels to enroll in graduate school in Santa Barbara, where I then resided for ten years. When you have lived in a city for a decade, even if you have been away for years, a return has the effect of collapsing time as you feel your way intuitively around familiar streets, parks, and landmarks. On this return I had stood on the steps of the Old Mission, the same steps where I had stood more than two decades previously with my religious studies professor.

These last two days the fog had burned off and the azure Pacific was vivid and bright. The large crowd was again filtering away from the mission steps, this time following the funeral service that had honored the memory of that same professor, my friend. These two days had been electric with returning memories of my graduate school decade, years in which my professor became my dissertation director, my spiritual companion, my children's godfather, and my friend: the two of us exulting in my graduate assistant's office over my first published article; buying apricot bonbons on a lark after a tedious colloquium; eating mashed potatoes in a suburban coffee shop as he joyfully anticipated the upcoming happy event that I, nauseated with morning sickness, was having difficulty appreciating; signing "good night" as we padded noiselessly to our respective cells during a class visit to a Trappist monastery; flipping through the Lutheran hymnal and pouncing upon the perfect hymn for the day, he playing, I singing; laboring over the footnotes for our book; him pacing the hospital halls and comforting my husband while I agonized in labor; finding a red rose on my doorstep after my dissertation defense; flinging ideas for a team-taught course across the garden pathway as I pushed my toddler's stroller and he jogged by on his afternoon exercise; joking in the university parking lot, weekday late afternoon, "Let's blow this fire trap. Let's go to Buellton!" Buellton, a small community a number of miles north of Santa Barbara, was the home of Anderson's Split Pea Soup. Billboards lining the road to the town advertise a cartoon Laurel and Hardy pair named "Split Pea" and "Hap-pea" stirring a huge cauldron of green sludge. Buellton has become a cipher for the endtimes. "When we get to Buellton," we joked. "Next year in Buellton," we promised, echoing the Jewish Passover promise of reunion in Jerusalem.

The memories spill one over the other as familiar sites pass by. Another decade has intervened since I resided in Santa Barbara, but my professor-friend and I never lost touch. Letters, phone calls, e-mail, and visits snatched from our respective busy schedules cemented our bond. It was especially at the annual meeting of the American Academy of Religion that we hoped to connect, although a few times one or the other of us didn't attend. The reunions were in different places: breakfast in a Chicago kosher deli; a late-afternoon drive through the Mendocino wine country; a repeated round-trip ride on the New Orleans ferry that carried restaurant and hotel employees out of the tourist district. Our meetings were a chance to touch base, to laugh, to catch up. Always they were rooted in what had originally brought us together—the common search, pursued through the discipline of religious studies, for the deep life, for the transparency of a life lived open to the presence of God.

Philadelphia was the site of one of our most wonderful reunions. About a month before the annual meeting, my mentor had sent a wry, witty note. It began, "Would Dr. Wright grace us with the pleasure of her company at an outing to the New Jerusalem?" About an hour outside the City of Brotherly Love is the international headquarters of the Swedenborgian Society. A seminary, cathedral, library archives, and extensive museum make up the compound. The Society, knowing the American Academy of Religion was to meet in Philadelphia, had invited a select group of scholars to an evening's outing, including dinner and a guided tour of the entire establishment. They wished scholars in the fields of alternative religions or the phenomenology of religion to become familiar with research opportunities available to them. Should we take a bus ride and have dinner with the Swedenborgians? It seemed too delightful an opportunity to resist.

I did a little homework before we went. Emanuel Swedenborg was an early-eighteenth-century scientist who had spent a lifetime working at the Swedish government's Board of Mines. He was also an incredibly creative intellect, having anticipated in his scientific inquiries nebular theory, magnetic theory, and the airplane. His inventions were many. Swedenborg's inquiring mind had a mystical bent as well. He was the son of a Lutheran bishop who was also a professor of theology and scripture at Uppsala University, and a sense of the spiritual dimension of things compelled him. He attempted to show by scientific analysis that the universe had a fundamental spiritual structure. In midlife he experienced what he described as the direct consciousness of angels as well as the spiritual realm in normal life, and he felt commissioned to make his ideals known. Out of this came the idea of the New Church, a spiritual fraternity of all those of various ecclesial allegiances who accepted his doctrines. Central to Swedenborg's vision was belief in the intimate correspondence between the physical and spiritual worlds. In what is perhaps his greatest work, *The Apocalypse Revealed*, the Swedish mystic plumbed the scriptures to cull out a unique spiritual vision of their inner meaning. He rejected the doctrine of the Trinity; instead, he avowed that God is one in three principles (love, divine wisdom, and divine energy), each manifest in Jesus Christ. The New Jerusalem is symbolic of the ideal human society, which will become manifest as all human beings accept and practice the spiritual truths revealed in scripture. When this occurs, Jesus will make his second coming in Spirit, not in person.

Saturday night of the annual meeting we met with the other scholars and our tour guides and boarded a chartered van for the ride out to the Swedenborgian headquarters. A number in the group were of Scandinavian origin and my mentor, in typical fashion, got us singing the old hymns from the Lutheran hymnal: songs of longing for home, for the completion of all things.

The evening turned out to be an utterly magical one. The Swedenborgian headquarters was nestled in a Pennsylvania valley settled exclusively by society members a century before. Hills cupped the community of the New Jerusalem, verdant lawns flocked with late autumn-leafed trees swept between members' homes. Nestled in the cup's bottom was the magnificent Cathedral of Bryn Athyn, a huge, northern-European Gothic structure constructed according to the spiritual architectural principles of Emanuel Swedenborg. Bryn Athyn contains no straight lines, for the mystic scientist had observed that nature, which is revelatory of spirit, has no straight lines. Only natural materials had been used, dark hardwood and gleaming granite especially. All the walls were slightly convex and the cathedral floor had a rise of almost a foot from the front doors to the altar. Everything was exquisitely hand carved with vegetative designs. And the place was saturated in symbols from Revelation. Around the altar loomed seven golden candlesticks, the ambo was carved all around with jewel-like imagery of the city-bride and the Lamb's banquet, stained glass shimmered with depictions of the promised new earth.

Our guide led us from the cathedral to the seminary library where the Swedenborg archives are housed. There the mystic scientist's astonishing mind revealed itself, his painstaking observations and calculations of the physical universe having yielded affirmations of the spiritual substructure sustaining and shaping all that is. Finally, we were escorted to a nearby Scottish baronial castle, former home of a Society member who had made his fortune in the nineteenth century in plate glass. Formerly the residence for a bustling family, the castle had been deeded to the Society and kept as headquarters and museum for the vast collection of ancient treasures the plate-glass baron had collected over the years. After a brief, informative lecture by our hosts, we dined in the commodious anteroom of the castle, where the massive stone walls were hung with medieval tapestries. Then we toured the upper chambers, home to Assyrian friezes, Greek statuary, Roman pottery, Egyptian artifacts; and the lower chambers, display area for a breathtaking collection of medieval European stained glass. My mentor-friend and I were swept up in the numinousness of it all: the dark, star-canopied valley; the glittering vision of the New Jerusalem nestled peacefully among the hills; the strange and

magical antiquity of this turreted Scottish castle. Our tour took us to an upper balcony that overlooked the surroundings. The carpet of lights that was
Philadelphia winked at us from across a dark distance. We lingered behind
our group a bit, savoring the evening's stillness, then crept back into the cor-
nucopia of castle rooms, finding ourselves finally in a small, round music conservatory just large enough for a foot-pumped organ and a few chairs. Several
Swedenborgian hymnals lay about, and letting our tour group move ahead of
us once more, my mentor and I flipped through the pages.

"Shall we?" he queried, sitting down at the keyboard.

"Yes," I readily replied. And we found a familiar melody, with lyrics somewhat altered to reflect the Society's theological perspective, and he began to
play as I sang.

As we emerged from the conservatory, a fellow visitor stuck his head through
the doorway. "I can't believe it. Where was that coming from? I thought I
heard angels singing," he breathed. We smiled, for we knew in some strange
way what he thought was true.

On the bus ride home we gloried together about our strange and wondrous evening, how we had sung our way through the Lutheran hymnbook to
the New Jerusalem, and how it shone and with what beauty, and how we had
felt there the deep springs of our long friendship well up and overflow. The
convergence of heaven and earth. Later we would half-joke about the New
Jerusalem. But we knew we were really talking about the exquisitely beautiful
and powerful longing for God that stretched tight beneath everything we did
and were.

It had even come up in an e-mail I sent to him Wednesday, October 22.

Fall has fallen. Sleet and snow today. Heading out of town to Missouri
for a pastoral gathering tomorrow. Thinking of you deciding all those
things, meeting everyone halfway on everything. It will be different in
the New Jerusalem. I trust it will also be equally interesting.

He replied on Thursday, October 28:

Because e-mail was down I just read this message this morning before
departing for D.C. Thanks so much for your understanding. Hope
Nebraska warms up.

That same evening a mutual friend phoned to inform me that my mentor-
friend had collapsed from a heart attack in the Washington Dulles International Airport and had died. The funeral was held at the Old Mission, his
residence and my former hometown. I stood on the steps overlooking the
azure Pacific where the two of us had stood twenty-three years before. It had

come full circle. His wife and eldest daughter had asked me to sing at the service. I was sent a copy of a short hymn he had composed as a young man of eighteen. His music, my voice once more. The date was Monday, November 3, just following All Saints' and All Souls' days.

The music and scripture for the festal days extended themselves into the funeral service. The choir sang:

> For all the saints who from their labors rest,
> All who by faith before the world confessed,
> Your name, O Jesus, be forever blest.
> Alleluia! Alleluia![47]

And we listened to the reading from Revelation:

> Then I saw a new heaven and a new earth; for the first heaven and the first earth had passed away, and the sea was no more. And I saw the holy city, the new Jerusalem, coming down out of heaven from God, prepared as a bride adorned for her husband, And I heard a loud voice from the throne saying,
> > "See, the home of God is among mortals.
> > He will dwell with them as their God;
> > they will be his peoples,
> > and God himself will be with them;
> > he will wipe every tear from their eyes.
> > Death will be no more;
> > mourning and crying and pain will be no more
> > for the first things have passed away."
> And the one who was seated on the throne said, "See, I am making all things new." Also he said, "Write this, for these words are trustworthy and true." Then he said to me, "It is done! I am the Alpha and the Omega, the beginning and the end. To the thirsty I will give water as a gift from the spring of the water of life." (Rv 21:1-6, New Revised Standard Version)

Imagination matters. The way we imagine the last things shapes our present. How we image God both articulates our deepest dreaming and fashions our capacity to dream. What we dream together unleashes us for love.

Heart of Flame and Fire

The Hearts of Jesus and Mary
and the Eucharistic Pelican
Embroidery by
Madeleine Sophie Barat
Late eighteenth century

Boundless Love! I plunge into your fire and the flames that fill all creation so I might love you in all places in everything. Jesus, I offer you all the boundless love of your Sacred Heart, the Heart of your Father and the Heart of your Mother, and all the hearts that love you in heaven and on earth. How I long for the universe to be transformed into flaming fires of love for you.

—John Eudes, 1601-1680

Missionary. Not to an exotic foreign land. The first flush of colonizing and conquest abroad had abated. This was, after all, the middle of the seventeenth century. The mission field was now native. John Eudes and his generation, loosely knit members of that spiritual tradition known as the French School, set out to evangelize the people of France. For Eudes, Normandy was the primary mission field.

Preaching and prayer were his tools as an evangelist. The persuasion of the heart. And so he preached. And so he prayed. And so he composed hymns and antiphons. Introits and benedictions. Matins, vespers and lauds. A mass text in 1668. So the people could be persuaded. Enfolded really. In the performative rituals of liturgy. At daybreak, open their eyes and lips and sing forth the heart's praise. At noon, rest in adoration. At nightfall, nestle into the divine embrace.

> Jesus, Lord, thank you for that astonishing gift—
>   your heart.
>
> Your heart showers me with such gifts.
>
> God of my heart, be always the center of my life.
>
> My heart's God, my love, Jesus always.

Heart of Jesus, my rule and my guide.

O my Heart, when I shelter you, I shelter everything
       that is.

Gentle humble Jesus, have mercy.

O sweet, sad Love enthroned
Upon the Cross, the Martyr's King.
Teach us your music: your cross the joyful sound
The crown and glory we sing.

Hearts of Mary and of Jesus, my most loving heart![48]

Always, for Eudes, it was the heart. The hearts of the people. The heart of
the preacher. The hearts of Mary and Jesus. Eudes is credited with writing
the first book on the devotion and articulating the first real theology of the
Sacred Heart. He did so by interpreting the devotion against the backdrop of
Catholic teachings about the Trinity and salvation, stressing that devotion to
any aspect of Jesus (for example, his heart) implied worship of Christ and the
entire Godhead. He specified the Sacred Heart devotion as love for God lost
because of human sin yet restored through grace expressed in the sacraments.
Within this theologically orthodox framework, Eudes went on to focus on
the human encounter with God through the affections. The heart of Jesus
and the heart of the believer became one.

> Yes, this admirable Heart is mine. It is mine because the Eternal Father
> has given it to me; it is mine because the Blessed Virgin has given it to
> me; it is mine because [Christ] himself has given it to me, not only to be
> my refuge and shelter in my needs, to be my oracle and my treasure, but
> also to be the model of my life and of my actions. I wish to study this
> rule constantly so as to follow it faithfully.[49]

By the middle of the seventeenth century what had been a diffuse if ubiquitous devotion to the heart came into theological and liturgical focus. Francis
de Sales had laid the groundwork for this to the extent that his richly varie-
gated vision of the Christian life centered on the symbol of the heart. Francis
was an early figure in the French Catholic reform, that remarkable surge of
spiritual vitality and creativity that erupted during the seventeenth century.

But Francis was only one luminary, an early one, among many in the reform; Bérulle, Condren, Olier, Vincent de Paul, and Eudes are names that
recall the era, the so-called French School. (Francis de Sales is seen as a fore-
runner rather than a member of the school and Vincent de Paul as the founder
of his own tradition.) Characteristics of the French School included a sense of

the grandeur of God and the "nothingness" of the human person, adherence to the "states" of Jesus, devotion to the Virgin Mary, intense apostolic mission, ecclesial loyalty, and eucharistic adoration. Beyond this, each reformer gave to the Christian life a distinctive face.

For John Eudes, that face was heart shaped. In his youth Eudes trained with the Jesuits, then entered the French Oratory, the society of reforming priests founded by Bérulle. His intense apostolic labors included working among plague victims, establishing a refuge for recovering prostitutes, erecting Confraternities of the Sacred Heart both inside and outside of seminaries, founding an associate program for laity (the Society of the Heart of the Mother Most Admirable), preaching no fewer than one hundred missions, mostly throughout northern France, and (after leaving the Oratory) establishing the Society of Jesus and Mary (known as the Eudists) for the education of priests and missionary work and the Congregation of Our Lady of Charity (for religious women).

Eudes is unique among members of the French School for his marked emphasis on the symbol of the heart. That emphasis originated in his own devotion to the heart of Mary and then extended to a consideration of the heart of her Son. These considerations were not merely devotional in the private sense of the word but were directed outward with characteristic missionary zeal. The French religious renewal spearheaded by the Eudists carried the good news of God's incredible love for humankind. The Sacred Heart was the supreme symbol of that love.

The language of love that Eudes preached and that flowed from his pen is among the most affective and attractive in the tradition. For him, the heart was warmth, a contagious kindling of fire and flame. The divine fire was infinite and unbounded. His theology was poetic. His liturgies were fiery love letters that carried Love's longing heart to heart.

Jesus' heart loves boundlessly. The uncreated, divine love which fills that heart is, quite simply, God's own self. Because God is unlimited, God's love is also unlimited. Since God is everywhere, God's love is everywhere, in all places and things. The Sacred Heart loves us not only in heaven but on earth. In the sun, the stars, in everything created. We are loved in all the hearts in heaven, we are loved in the hearts of everyone on earth who has some care for us. All the love in heaven and on earth shares in the love of Jesus' Sacred Heart. Jesus even loves us in our enemies' hearts. I say boldly that we are loved even in hell, in the hearts of the damned and demons, in spite of their anger and hatred, because divine love is everywhere, filling heaven and earth like the presence of God.[50]

The first generations of Protestant reformers certainly had no patience with the baroque, even rococo, visualizations of the heart that pervaded Catholic Christendom. But the verbal imagery associated with the tradition did surface in later streams of Christianity identified with the reform.

Seventeenth- and eighteenth-century European religious life on both sides of the Protestant-Catholic divide has, in fact, been described under the rubric of the religion of the heart.[51] What characterized these "religions"—whether the baroque Catholic movements of Quietism or Sacred Heart devotion, English Puritan or Scots-Irish Revivalism, the Quakers, Lutheran or Reformed Pietism, the Moravians or Early Methodism—was not their doctrinal heterodoxy (they were mostly movements within established traditions) but their insistence that the true meeting point between God and humankind was in the "heart," that is, in the will and affections. In these heart traditions, affective experience was central to lived Christian faith.

A subtle shift in the spiritual meaning of the term *heart* had occurred. If medieval theologians and spiritual writers had thought of the heart as comprehending both the affective and intellectual aspects of human life, early modern Christians, especially but not exclusively in the Protestant world, began to equate the heart solely with the affections and the will. The heart could then be contrasted with the head (intellect). For many in this period, true Christianity consisted primarily in an affective change of heart.

Scholars have offered a number of explanations for the emergence of these affective religious sentiments in the early modern era. One of the most convincing suggests that Europeans of all denominations were wearied by the century of warfare and denominational and intradenominational quarrels that followed the Reformation. All intractable warring sides had appealed to the objective, publicly accessible authorities of the Bible and church tradition. Disgusted by the visible failure of Christianity to provide the basis of a stable society, some rejected religious authority altogether and looked instead to human reason to guide civic life. Thus the Enlightenment was born. Others, unwilling to reject religious tradition, turned inward to a more individual and subjective appropriation of the Christian faith. They turned to affective piety, to the human heart. Thus were born the so-called religions of the heart.

This sort of piety flourished most in the varied offshoots of the Protestant reform. It can be seen clearly in the pan-European movement known as Pietism, which originated in the United Provinces, spread through the Reformed churches, and flowered in its most notable form in Lutheran churches in the late seventeenth century. Essential to the Lutheran synthesis was the influence of Johann Arndt (1555-1621), who insisted that Christians should be schooled in a practical living faith rather than doctrinal controversies. Arndt's *True Christianity* outlined a vision of union with God that was not mystical but ethical and affective, focusing as it did on a union with God through love and will.

> Perfection is not, as some think, a high, great, spiritual, heavenly joy and meditation, but it is a denial of one's own will, love, honor, a knowledge of one's nothingness, a continual completion of the will of God, a burning love for neighbor, a heart-held compassion, and, in a word, a love that desires, thinks and seeks nothing other than God alone insofar as this is possible in the weakness of this life.[52]

Arndt was a decided influence on Philip Jacob Spener (1635-1705), author of *Pia Desideria* and the most identifiable name in the Pietist movement. Spener was in turn an influence on August Hermann Francke (1663-1727). Young Francke's conversion experience, prompted by his inability to preach on the Johannine text "these are written that you may believe that Jesus is the Christ, the Son of God, and that believing you may have life in his name," became exemplary of the heartfelt, experiential faith central to Pietism.

> Then the Lord God heard me, the living God from his holy throne, as I was still on my knees. So great was his fatherly love that he would not take away such doubt and restlessness of heart little by little, with which I would have been quite content, but rather he suddenly heard me so that I would be all the more convinced and would bridle my strayed reason, to use nothing against his power and faithfulness; thus he suddenly heard me. Then, as one turns his head [in a twinkling], so all my doubts were gone; I was sure in my heart of the grace of God in Jesus Christ; I knew God not only as God, but rather as one called my Father. All sadness and unrest in my heart was taken away in a moment. On the contrary, I was suddenly so overwhelmed as with a stream of joy that I praised out of the high spirits the God who had shown me such grace. I arose again of a completely different mind then when I had knelt down.[53]

A form of the archetypal conversion experience discovered in the later Evangelical revival is evident here. Where Lutheran Arndt's description of union of divine and human hearts—which parallels his Catholic contemporary Francis de Sales's dictum "Live Jesus"—focused on transformation of the heart through disciplined, loving conformity of wills, Francke's account imagines the change of heart in dramatic subjective terms. Gone is the imaginative shape and texture of the divine heart. Instead, the affective human experience of divine condescension alone remains.

The vivid imagery of Jesus' suffering heart, so powerfully explored in earlier centuries, was not completely absent from Protestant piety, however.

Pietism was one stream of influence that fed into the spirituality of the Moravian church. This small but influential Christian group, which is the first instance in the tradition of nondenominational Evangelical movements attempting to avoid sectarian controversy, was watered by a variety of sources: Lutheran Orthodoxy, Pietism, Jansenism, the "Bohemian Brethren" remnant of the ancient Unitas Fratrum, and Reformed and Anglican piety. From these eclectic streams developed an ecumenical conception of a united Protestant church. Interestingly, it was the Moravians who retained the colorful medieval devotion to the suffering Christ. The wounds, the blood, the pierced heart reverberate through Moravian hymnody and theological reflection.

Nicholas Ludwig, Count von Zinzendorf (1700-1760) was crucial in the complex, experimental development of what was to become the Moravian church. The irreducible quality of inner religious conviction in Zinzendorf is rooted in an almost mystical incorporation of the truth of the Savior's suffering body. Placed before the meditative eye of the beholder, the heat of the suffering heart of Christ melts the human heart as if it were wax before a fire.

> This is the first part of *fides explicita*. One knows in his inmost person with whom he deals. One knows him from head to foot, in heart and body. One knows him in his most profound nature as it is now and was then. And when one has thought and felt this long enough and has arranged it in all possible drawers of the mind and has become a scribe instructed for the kingdom of Heaven, then one takes out one truth after the other, presents it and demonstrates it with reasons grounded deep within oneself, which grasp the hearers' hearts. For if one would speak to those who know and love the Savior about his glory and majesty, then they say, "There is no doubt about that; that is clear enough to me, and I have no hesitation here. But the trembling of God shakes my soul. His suffering, his death, his anxiety, his atoning-battle which he endured for me, the fact that he had to be absolved through the Holy Spirit for my sake, that with him all my sin is forgiven, that with him I have leave to be eternally blessed—this is the reality for which no word, no expression is adequate." One's feeling of this cannot be made plain to someone who does not have it himself. It all gets stuck or comes out only half and half. These are the *arrheta rhemata*, the unspeakable things.

> When the heart confronts my eye
> In all his godly greatness,
> Then I think, "I die!"
> To gauge again that greatness,
> According to his humanity,

> No heart can be so small,
> So weak no other ever can be,
> As this heart at all.
> Then I think: Good-bye,
> You self-empowered repenting.
> Like wax before the fire, I
> Want to melt in Jesus' suffering.
> My heart shall see the wrath
> In this suffering, pain,
> And see the cleansing bath
> For all my transgressions' stain.

When a person has this faith, this faith-in-distress, this faith made doubt-ful by reason of great unworthiness, this faith which has fallen in love through the real help, through the blessed happiness and grace which the heart has obtained, is that not beautiful? When a person has within himself the meditations of faith and the lasting feeling, the searching in Jesus even up to his eternal Godhead, finding his Father and his spirit, and all this coming from his side, out of his heart, is that not beautiful? And when he at last has, experiences, and obtains as a gift the learned faith which preaches from the wounds of Jesus to his Creator's power and from his Creator's power into the side of Jesus, into his wounded heart, and which makes everybody convinced and wise and brings them to an evidence and demonstrative certainty, is that not beautiful? Is that not a great blessedness? Does that not make a blessed man who, as Paul says, believes all this from his heart (Rom. 10:9) and can say and confess it with a plerophory [subjective complete assurance]? His faith so flows from his heart that he can thus pour himself out before mankind.[54]

Religion, for Zinzendorf, consisted of a personal relationship with the Savior effected through a re-created heart and imagined as a mystical marriage. Christ was the "true and eternal husband with whom we must be so united (by faith and love) that we can no longer see or hear anything else above or beyond him, that we and He remain inseparably together."[55]

Moravian piety in its turn fed into the converging currents of the heart tradition that emerged in the eighteenth century in the form of the Evangeli-cal revival. Against philosophical trends, of which deism or skepticism are examples, a pan-denominational tendency to reduce Christian life to moral improvement, and the social transitions of urbanization and industrialization, this revival moved like wildfire through the Christian world—from Wales, through England, and across the Atlantic Ocean to American shores. Closely associated with that oceanic transit are John (1703-1791) and Charles Wesley

(1707-1788), Anglican priests and founders of the Methodist movement. It was aboard a ship bound for Georgia that the Wesley brothers met a company of Moravian pilgrims and were moved by their heartfelt piety.

In Georgia, the Wesley brothers came into contact with proponents of Lutheran Pietism in the tradition of Spener and Francke. Back home they continued their converse with London Moravians, who pressed them on the question of whether they had experienced the assurance of pardon that Pietism stressed. On Pentecost Sunday, 1738, Charles found his assurance. Three days later, John did as well. In his journal he described the culmination of this long spiritual search in the now legendary "heartwarming" experience.

> In the evening I went very unwillingly to a society in Aldersgate Street, where one was reading Luther's Preface to the Epistle to the Romans. About a quarter before nine, while he was describing the change God works in the heart through faith in Christ, I felt my heart strangely warmed. I felt I did trust in Christ, Christ alone for salvation, and an assurance was given me that he had taken away *my* sins, even *mine*, and saved *me* from the law of sin and death.[56]

John's response to this transformation of heart was increased evangelical activity: preaching, establishing varieties of small-group structures for the spiritual nurture of people in various life circumstances, and spiritual development. Charles's response was to write hymns. This lesser-known Wesley has, in fact, more deeply impressed the imaginative consciousness of Christianity than his better-known brother. Charles's hymnody was prodigious. He created a body of hymns for use not only throughout the seasons of the liturgical year but throughout the spiritual life cycle. In fact, the first Methodist hymnals were uncustomarily arranged according to the progress and affective peaks and valleys of the evangelically conceived spiritual journey. One of the most familiar to modern ears is the following adaptation of Wesley's classic "O for a Heart to Praise My God." In it are lyrical echoes of the ancient yet familiar tradition of the heart:

> O for a heart to praise my God,
> A heart from sin set free,
> A heart that always feels thy blood
> So freely shed for me.
>
> A heart resigned, submissive, meek,
> My great Redeemer's throne,
> Where only Christ is heard to speak,
> Where Jesus reigns alone.

Oh! for a lowly, contrite heart,
Believing true and clean;
Which neither life nor death can part
From him that dwells within.

A heart in everything renewed,
And full of love divine
Perfect and right, and pure, and good,
A copy, Lord, of thine.

Thy gracious nature, Lord, impart;
Come quickly from above,
Write thy new name upon my heart,
Thy new best name of love!

Exchange

"Margaret Mary"
Br. Michael McGrath, O.S.F.S.

Exchange

What is the weight
  of the heart you promise
  in exchange
  for the stone's weight
    that lives inside me now?
What is the width
  of mercy plundered
  if my heart's walls
    are breached?
What is the depth
  of joy discovered
  as I am poured out
    of myself?
What is the length
  of love learned

in the prints left
　　where you walked?
What is the breadth
　of freedom given
　when my shoulders
　　bear your yoke?
And what is the weight, width,
　　depth, length, height, breadth,
　　of sorrow
I will hold in the taking?[58]

Margaret Mary, you terrible, wonderful creature. Lauded as the Apostle of the Sacred Heart. Maligned by one contemporary commentator on religion as neurotic, masochistic, guilty of wish fulfillment, and imprisoned in a pious projection,[59] you nevertheless have been the object of admiration and regard for over three centuries. Rightly so, for it was your visions, received in the intimacy of prayer in an obscure convent in the provincial French backwater of Paray-le-Monial, that eventually gave shape to the official devotional cult of the Sacred Heart. The nineteenth- and early-twentieth-century church venerated you, enamored as it was by the otherworldly religiosity of consumptive virgins, child martyrs, and spiritual victimhood. You gave them suffering and self-annihilation and unworthiness in spades.

You certainly are not an easy figure for the faithful of twenty-first century America to decode. You entered the Visitation convent of Paray-le-Monial in 1674, when you were just twenty-four, against your mother's wishes and armed for religious life with only a lonely, abusive childhood and the burning desire to belong completely to your beloved Jesus. It's that part of you I find compelling. The unquenchable thirst for God alone. The white-hot desire to burn away anything in yourself that stood between you and the living flame of Love.

If social anthropologists are correct in pointing out that often it is the marginal people who offer the most permeable membrane through which emergent ideas in the form of visionary revelations are offered to a society, then Margaret Mary is a case in point. She was nobody's poster child until later in her life. Then she was honored mainly within her community. Her international visibility occurred gradually and only after her death.

Her autobiography, penned under obedience to a religious superior and left unfinished when his term of office expired, reads like a distillation of earlier pious hagiography: a vow of chastity made at the age of four, her horror of marriage, an unbidden illness cured by a vow of consecration to the Virgin Mary, domestic persecution, a transposition of her personal suffering to the suffering of Christ, self-reproach at her perceived sinfulness, repugnance at ordinary eating and a hunger for the eucharist, a struggle against the life her family envisioned for her, liberation into the enclosure of the monastery, alienation and misunderstandings within her community, the punishment of suspicious superiors, the intensifying refuge of prayer, locutions, visions, and impassioned exchanges between herself and Jesus.

Between the lines a reader can discern the singular religiosity of a young woman who had in her solitary visits to church in childhood (which the relatives who kept her and her mother under virtual house arrest suspected were fabricated to meet young men) cultivated a remarkable sense of the presence of God. This was no vague, spiritual presence but a living, breathing, highly emotive, and intensely communicative relationship. This relationship reached its apogee in 1673 on December 29, the Feast of John the Beloved Disciple, when Margaret Mary received the first of the "great revelations" that later came to structure the cult of the Sacred Heart.

Once when I was before the blessed sacrament, (I had found a little space of time, though the work I had been given left me little), I was suddenly completely surrounded by the divine presence. It was so intense I lost my sense of who and where I was. I abandoned myself to the Spirit, yielding my heart to the power of his love. He made me rest for a long time on his divine breast where he showed me the marvels of his love and the unspeakable secrets of his sacred heart that had always been hidden before. He opened them to me there for the first time, in such a real and tangible way. Even though I am always afraid of deceiving myself about what I say happens inside me, I could not doubt what was happening because of the effects that the grace produced in me. This is what seemed to me to happen:

He said to me "My divine heart is so impassioned with love for humanity, and for you especially, it cannot contain the flames of its burning charity inside. It must spread them through you, and show itself to humanity so that they may be enriched by the previous treasures that I share with you, treasures which have all the sanctifying and saving graces needed to draw them back from the abyss of destruction. I have chosen you as an abyss of unworthiness and ignorance to accomplish this great work so that everything will be done by me."

Afterwards, he asked for my heart. I begged him to take it and he did, placing it in his own adorable heart. He let me see it there like a little atom consumed in a burning furnace. Then he returned it to me as a burning heart-shaped flame, and placed it where it had been, saying, "Here is a precious token of my love, my beloved. This will enclose a tiny spark of living flame within your side. It will serve as your heart and consume you until your last moment. Its intensity will be so unyielding that you will be unable to find relief, except briefly by bleeding. I will mark it so with the blood of my cross that it will bring you more humiliation and suffering than comfort. That is why I want you to ask for it in all simplicity, so that you can practice what is asked of you and be given the joy of shedding your blood on the cross of humiliation. And to prove that the grace I have just given is not imaginary and is the foundation of all the others I intend to give you, the pain in your side will always remain, even though I have closed the wound. If up until now you have only been called my slave, I now give you the name 'Beloved Disciple of My Sacred Heart.'"[60]

The following year saw two more of her "great revelations." The fourth and final occurred in June of 1675. If in the first the Visitandine experienced an "exchange of hearts" and received the appellation "beloved disciple," in the subsequent visions her newly acquired identity and mission were fleshed out dramatically. She was to promulgate the following devotional practices: eucharist on the First Friday of every month in honor of the Sacred Heart; a nightly hour of prostrated adoration between Thursday and Friday in memory of Christ's agony in the Garden; and most significantly, the institution of a yearly feast of the Sacred Heart placed on the Friday following the Feast of Corpus Christi (the Body of Christ). The sentiment that fueled her aspiration was given to her by Jesus himself.

Jesus, my sweet master, presented himself to me, all splendid with glory, His Five Wounds shining like so many suns. Flames issued . . . especially from his Adorable Bosom, which looked like an open furnace and revealed to me His most loving and lovable Heart . . . "If only they would make Me some return for my love."[61]

Margaret Mary clearly was not the inventor of the Sacred Heart devotion. Centuries of private devotional practice all over Christendom had paved the way. Moreover, the Visitation order she joined was heir to the heart theology of Francis de Sales and Jane de Chantal. Yet, strangely enough, when as a young professed she began to introduce intentional devotion to the heart in her community, it was viewed as a foreign and suspect practice. This type of devotion was apparently not known in the provinces; certainly it was not known to her sisters in religion at Paray.

Moreover, visionary experience itself was keenly suspect at this period of French history. Public quarrels over Quietism and Jansenism had signaled the end of easy acceptance in the church for anything that looked like individual mystical or spiritual experience. The favor of the day was given to doctrinal orthodoxy, belief in the sufficiency of the sacraments, and loyalty to ecclesiastical authority. Add to this cultural mistrust of individual illumination the fact that by the end of the seventeenth century the Visitation Order came to stress the dimension of its charism that emphasized humble, simple conformity to the community rule, and there was even more reason for Margaret Mary (who couldn't be trusted to mind the monastery livestock because she let them wander off while she went into a rapture) to be under suspicion.

It took Jesuit Claude de la Columbière (1641-1682) to authenticate her visions both for herself and, obliquely, for her community. It has not been unusual for spiritually gifted women in the church to find champions in some male counterpart. Indeed, this is the norm rather than the exception. Claude had been assigned as confessor for Margaret Mary's monastery. His Jesuit community at Paray, like the Visitation, had a few decades prior been established as part of the militant reestablishment of Catholic ascendancy in the region. A generation past, the area had been economically and socially dominated by Huguenot families. These French Protestants were expelled by Louis XIV's revocation of the Edict of Nantes, which had allowed French Protestantism to coexist alongside its Catholic counterpart. The Jesuit Colombière, himself steeped in the Sacred Heart devotion, which his order had long encouraged, discovered in this obscure provincial nun a friend and fellow spirit traveler. It was he who deemed Margaret Mary's visions to be direct communiqués from God, and he whose retreat notes, read aloud much later in the refectory at Paray, suggested to Margaret Mary's community that something graced and extraordinary had indeed occurred among them. Eventually, the Paray-le-Monial monastery found common purpose in initiating and promoting the Sacred Heart devotion under the aspect revealed to Margaret Mary Alacoque. The devotion was simultaneously promoted by others outside the cloister, especially Jesuit Fathers Croiset and Gallifet, whose writings were widely circulated.[62]

Margaret Mary's visions emphasized the devotional postures of adoration and reparation. Adoration was due the heart that loved humankind with such abundance yet had suffered so for that love. The attitude of adoration was impressed upon Margaret Mary with the force of vision:

> Another time, when the Sisters were working in common, picking hemp, I withdrew into a small courtyard near the Blessed Sacrament where, doing my work on my knees, I felt myself wholly rapt in interior and exterior recollection, and at the same time, the Adorable Heart of my Jesus appeared to me brighter than the sun. It was surrounded by the flames of Its pure love and encircled by Seraphim who sang in marvelous harmony: "Love triumphs, love enjoys, the love of the Sacred Heart rejoices!" These blessed spirits invited me to unite with them in praising the Divine Heart.[63]

The Seraphic visitors, in fact, urged the visionary to form an association with them for the purpose of adoration, a devotional association that later was extended to members of her community. Adoration was not the sole prescribed posture however. The association was to be linked with reparation. The Jesus who made himself so corporeally known to the Paray Visitandine was both sorrowful and displeased with the response of the people for whom he had suffered. Margaret Mary's sense of sin was acute. She agonized over her own sinfulness, the sinfulness of the Paray sisterhood, and the sinfulness of French society. As keen as her personal sense of unworthiness was, it was swallowed up in the new identity of disciple given to her in the mystical "exchange of hearts" that inaugurated her "great revelations." Part of her mission was to make reparation for the sinful indifference of others toward the heart of the Savior. In the last of the "great revelations" that shaped the perimeters of the liturgical devotion, Jesus specified this mission.

> Being before the Blessed Sacrament one day of its octave, I received from my God tokens of his love, and felt urged to make Him some return, and of rendering Him love for love. "You cannot make me a greater return of love," He said, "than by doing what I have so often asked you." Then, showing me His Divine Heart, He said: "Behold this Heart, which has loved humankind so much, that it has spared Itself nothing, even to the point of exhausting and consuming Itself in order to show them Its love; and in return I receive from most only ingratitude through their irreverence and sacrileges, as well as through the coldness and contempt in which they hold the Sacrament of Love."[64]

The eucharistic focus of the visions is clear. And the layered implications of the Visitandine's sightings are striking. To put it rather bluntly, these were politically charged visions.

On the first level, they spoke directly to Margaret Mary herself—of her vocation, her identity, her mission. On a second level, the visions implicated the sisters at Paray-le-Monial. In fact, within a short time Margaret Mary was ordered by her invisible companion to confront her own monastery about the tepidness of its religiosity—an order that, when carried out, did not endear the visionary to her sisters.

But the Sacred Heart revelations implied a wider audience than these few provincial cloistered women. Implied were broader ecclesial and societal challenges: Protestantism, Jansenism, and Quietism, as well as the growing religious skepticism that had permeated French intellectual life. The Sacred Heart eventually came to be the standard carried into battle by the French Catholic monarchy against all the enemy forces that threatened its foundations and its right to exist.[65]

Of course, this was a complex, lengthy journey. Later in her life Margaret Mary (prompted again by her divine mentor) proposed that the French monarch—none other than the absolutist Sun King, Louis XIV—put himself and the French realm under the patronage of the Sacred Heart. The message seems not to have reached the king. The marriage of the Sacred Heart symbol and the French people, however, had begun.

In the photo my tiny, black-tufted infant head peeps out of a swath of blanket. Cradled by my handsome young father, we are surrounded by a small phalanx of well-wishers lined up against the church doors: Grandma Mae, wrapped in a fur-collared coat; Cousin Elsie, sporting a chic "pillbox" hat and stylish cashmere suit; Uncle Fred, wearing a suit that registers dark on the black-and-white film; the Reverend Allan Hunter, the lean, ascetic-looking pastor of First Congregational; and my mother, dressed in a floral print, the large black saucer of her hat framing her face like an art deco halo. Christening day.

My parents chose First Congregational for this ritual moment because of Pastor Hunter. He and my father had been compatriots in their conscientious objection during World War II, a rare enough company in any war, let alone that global conflict. In fact, my conception dates to the year just following the end of that war, when my father and others like him were returned to civilian life after serving in CO camps for the conflict's duration. My dad's contingent had been assigned to fight fires for the forest service.

So I was welcomed into the Christian community, sprinkled with the waters, on this particular shore, accompanied by doting relatives and bathed in the light of California sun and the radiance of Christian pacifism. That radiant legacy has followed me on all my religious peregrinations.

Besides the business of his contemporary jewelry workshop and retail store, my growing up was filled with the business of my father's interests in conflict resolution and nonviolence. There were out-of-town meetings that he attended and ground-breaking conferences of which I was only vaguely aware. He characterized it all as new and futuristic, for my father was as fascinated with the future as I, ironically, have been fascinated with the past.

I cannot claim that my father's motives in this search for peace were explicitly Christian. Pastor Hunter's were. That lean man was nurtured by the legacy of the historic peace churches—the Quakers and Mennonites—and nourished by prayerful reflection on the gospels. My father's motives were based more on common sense and were more direct. It was, in his eyes, the height of human folly to maim and kill for any ideal. To train to do so, in the armed services or elsewhere, was for him a nation's most myopic undertaking.

He would not have used the words of the spiritual, but he lived its uncompromising statement: "I ain't gonna study war no more."

My childhood memories are interspersed with images of Ban the Bomb marches and pamphleting passersby with manuals on the principles of conflict resolution. Martin Luther King Jr.'s witness, when it could penetrate consciousness beyond my immersion in little theater and the opposite sex, pervaded my adolescence. That witness continued to fuel my imagination when, as a college student, I joined an American Friends Summer Work Project in Luverne, Alabama, to help with voter registration among the disenfranchised poor black population in the rural South. It was during that 1967 summer that I heard King preach in his father's church in Atlanta. This was the first time that the profound Christian underpinnings of King's nonviolent political resistance were clear to me. They were more than clear. If ever in my life I have been present when the Spirit of God moved through a person and into a community, it was at Ebenezer Baptist that hot July Sunday.

Ritually brought to the waters of salvation, I was at the same time also baptized into the blood of the pacifist martyrs of the radical reformation and the blood of the American nation's own prophet of nonviolence.

Give us
A pure heart
That we may see thee,
A humble heart,
That we may hear thee,
A heart of love
That we may serve thee,
A heart of faith
That we may live thee.[66]

—Dag Hammarskjöld, twentieth century

Margaret Mary Alacoque was neither the first nor the last individual in the Catholic tradition to undergo an "exchange of hearts." A number of women in the medieval mystical tradition before her had encountered Jesus in a visionary or mystical mode and in the process "lost" their own hearts. The variants in the tradition were many, but inevitably the experience involved a visionary encounter and a hidden, interior transformation that the vision symbolized. Dorothy of Montau and Catherine de Ricci each received dramatic confirmation that her "old heart" was replaced by a "new heart." Dominican Margaret Ebner recounted a "grasp in the heart of an inner divine power" that impressed the "sweetest name" of Jesus within her.[67] Both Lutgard of

Awyieres and Catherine of Siena (whose experience was widely recounted and artistically represented) received Christ's own heart in place of their own.[68] This theme, of course, is part of the deep grammar of Christian prayer in which echoes Old Testament prayer, "Give me a clean heart," and the corresponding promise, "I will take away your heart of stone and replace it with a heart of flesh." The medieval cloister, luxuriating in the devotional imagery of the heart, vibrated with the songs of lover and beloved. What more fitting way for the radical imitation of Christ for which the tradition pressed than a mystical exchange of hearts? Paul's words "I no longer live but Christ lives in me" moved from metaphor to embodied understanding. Catherine's heart was "crushed"; Margaret Mary housed a spark of living flame. Other recipients of this curious (to modern sensibilities) grace each underwent the exchange their own unique ways.

But what of this exchange today? In what guise might this religious relic appear at the turn of the millennium? I find my own ruminations turning toward contemporary social theory, especially theories of nonviolent resistance that offer a vision of a transformed world that begins in a transformation of hearts.

It is especially the tradition of nonviolent resistance—articulated in the present century and culminating in the thinking of Martin Luther King Jr.— that seems to me to have the possibility of responding creatively to the violence so endemic in our present world.[69] King's theories provide the substructure beneath the various acts of civil disobedience that he and others orchestrated during his years as champion of civil rights for American blacks. The theories are significant not only because they analyze the structures that breed violence but also because they point to a radical change of heart that can potentially transform violence through the use of militant nonviolence.

Martin Luther King Jr. viewed militant nonviolence as the choice of the courageous. First, it was not a question of whether or not one should confront evil. He felt it was a fundamental human moral obligation to do so. The only choice one had was whether to resist violently or nonviolently. Second, the end sought by nonviolence was not victory over one's opponents but reconciliation with them based on the recognition of the common interests shared by all parties. For King, the goal was the creation of what he called the "beloved community," in which all would be reconciled. This implies that compromises must be made by all parties in order to find common ground. Third, the struggle for a just world was not a struggle against the impersonal forces of evil or against other people but against the structures of evil that enslave the oppressors as well as the oppressed. Thus revenge is foreign and forgiveness commonplace in King's vision of a transformed and transforming world. Fourth, one must be willing to accept suffering oneself rather than inflict suffering on others. Fifth, the resister must renounce both the use of physical violence and any internal spirit of violence. This inner conquest is perhaps the most difficult dimension of the nonviolent platform. One must genuinely love one's opponents, not because one approves of or even likes them, but because a fundamental agapic love has possessed one's heart. This agapic love is God's love for humans revealed most clearly in Jesus. Such love is a gift, a creative in-breaking of the Spirit that human beings cannot control but that can be courted by opening our hearts to grace. Sixth and finally, Martin Luther King Jr.'s theory of nonviolence assumes that there is cosmic companionship in the struggle for a just and loving world and that the true meaning of life is discovered in the personal effort to live humanely, courageously, and freely.

I would like to create a space, as it were, for the dialogue between the tradition of Sacred Heart devotion and nonviolent theory. It is clear to me that it is not enough simply to pray to the Sacred Heart of Jesus to take away the violence in contemporary culture. Nor do I think it is adequate for all of us simply to devote ourselves to making reparation for the sins of humankind, although this is an intercessory practice to which some may have a genuine call. Instead, I take my cue from the tradition of Margaret Mary and other women mystics who invite us to ask and prepare ourselves for an exchange of hearts. Our hearts must become inhabited by the heart of God. When it happened to Catherine of Siena, her heart was "crushed." Gertrude the Great describes the process as being "grasped." Francis de Sales, in less mystical fashion, simply enjoined Jesus to live and reign in human hearts. Margaret Mary experienced her heart as removed and replaced by a fiery atom. No matter how one might conceptualize this "exchange," it seems to me to be the fundamental dynamic both in King's vision and in the spirituality of the Sacred Heart.

What does it mean to experience this exchange? What are the aspects of a heart inhabited by the heart of God? First, I would say that the heart of God is embodied in the particular. The central, utterly stunning insight of the Christian religion is the idea of incarnation. As a historical and theological concept, the incarnation of God in human form is a familiar idea. But if we read the incarnation as a more wide-ranging symbol, a rich insight that invites us into a fundamental truth of existence, we see that the incarnation speaks of the conjunction of the visible and the invisible, the meeting of heaven and earth. Most specifically, it proclaims that spirit is discovered in matter, that the infinite is encountered precisely in the finite. This is not to be pantheistic, reducing God to the world, but to invite us into the paradox, to paraphrase Gerard Manley Hopkins's poem about the Virgin Mary, that infinity is cloistered in a dear womb. Her womb, our womb, the womb of the world.

What this means for us is that our hearts cannot be fixed on the generic or the ideal but must learn and exercise love through the particular. We are called to encounter God in the specific, embodied persons and events with which we come in contact. The extended tradition of contemplation on the Sacred Heart makes this abundantly clear. In much of that tradition the distinctive, bodily heart of Jesus is the focus. I have come to love the stunning fleshiness of it all, the sense that in gazing upon the organ itself one can know the depths of God. I admit it took me a long time to adjust to this concept and that originally I came to my study prepared to focus on the heart in a more conceptual manner. But the tradition is unambiguous. God does not love only with a free-floating, "spiritual" love but with the rush of blood, the tensing of muscle, with the tearing of tissue and bone. And so must we love.

To have a heart inhabited by God's heart, we must love specific people in all their idiosyncrasies. We must practice an energetically engaged love that mucks in the messiness of things. The medieval women mystics were so good at grasping this truth. For them, the God who died on the cross was as much a woman in childbirth as a sacrificial victim. God, for them, had the heart of a mother, whose love is inextricably linked to the irrepeatable flesh and blood of her child. To quote a famous passage by Julian of Norwich:

> But our true mother Jesus, he alone bears us for joy and for endless life, blessed may he be. So he carries us within him in love and travail, until the full time when he wanted to suffer the sharpest thorns and cruel pains that were ever or will be, and at the last he died. And when he had finished, and had borne us so for bliss, still all this could not satisfy his wonderful love.[70]

The God who bears us like a mother also loves us as one. God's open side becomes the mother's breast at which we suckle in search of nourishment to sustain our lives. Thus Catherine of Siena could explore her mystical understanding of the wounded side of Christ as God's nourishing breast:

> And just as a baby draws milk through its mother's breast, so souls in love with God draw God to themselves through Christ crucified. . . . Let your heart and soul burst with the health of love [as you drink] at this breast of charity through the flesh of Christ crucified.[71]

To have such a maternal heart ourselves means we must be lovers of all that is created, have our eyes opened to the deep spirit that slumbers within the substructure of rocks, courses through crystalline stream beds, and echoes in the oceans' primordial depths. Teilhard de Chardin, whose twentieth-century spiritual vision was contoured by loving gaze upon the Sacred Heart as well as by his scientific training, spoke of this reality in "My Litany":

> The world-zest
> The essence of all energy
> The cosmic curve
> The heart of God
> The issue of cosmogenesis
> The tide of cosmic convergence
> The God of evolution
> The universal Jesus . . .
> Focus of ultimate and universal energy
> Center of the cosmic sphere of cosmogenesis
> Heart of Jesus,
> heart of evolution,
> unite me to yourself.[72]

This incarnational intuition that the finite is the gateway to infinity (and its corollary that love can only be exercised in the particularity of finite persons and situations) dovetails well, I think, with the insights from nonviolent theory which insist that reconciliation and the creation of the beloved community is the end we seek. We cannot love our enemies if we cannot see them as potential friends, cannot find some vestige of humanity in them, cannot find God in all things as they are, even if we would wish them otherwise. To perceive the infinite in the finite requires an act of the imagination, a capacity to pierce stereotypes and appearances to reach the core of goodness that lingers in all created things. It requires enormous faith to suspend our own expectations and wait for God's illumination in the darkness. But that is what the embodied heart of God invites us to do.

The second revelatory insight in the tradition is that God's heart is the center where all paradoxes are held in tension. Christianity is a religion of paradoxes. Three in one. Fully God and fully human. Life born through death. These are foundational ideas that support the whole Christian edifice. The tradition of the Sacred Heart seems to me to be a vehicle through which we locate the place of paradoxical convergence. The heart is at the center of God's body, the center of the liturgy, the center of our redemption, and the center of the universe. There all things converge, but their convergence does not dilute distinctiveness into sameness. Instead, the incredible tension of holding opposites together generates intense creativity. For the center is not static but dynamic, and the existence of paradox there is not chaotic but life-giving. It is the ancient image of the divine heart as a fiery furnace that captures my imagination here and best expresses the creative potential of paradox. A passage from the life of Sister Margaret, a seventeenth-century Carmelite of Beaune, illuminates the creativity and dynamism of the furnace heart:

Thus He revealed His Heart as a vast and boundless furnace of love in which He enclosed her for days and nights. There were transfused so many graces at their source that her progress in perfection seemed greater in a single day than it had ever been for whole years at a stretch. That divine heart, searing like a hot fire, consumed her imperfections. . . . She noted the two-fold movement of dilation and compression of the Heart of Jesus, experienced by other saints, and understood that the Sacred Heart contracted as if to encompass the Holy Spirit, to love its Divine Father in His own name . . . and that the Sacred Heart expanded to shed abroad its Spirit . . . to communicate to His Mystical Body, the Church, all its vital warmth.[73]

Dilation and expansion, creative, dynamic movement. These are the qualities of God's own heart. So should they be ours. Nonviolent theory urges us in much the same direction.

Classically, nonviolent theory does not identify itself with any preconceived political or social agenda for it is not an ideology as much as an approach to life. It does not seek to push forward special interests as much as to arrive at the "beloved community" by whatever available nonviolent means. To have a heart thus fixed is to have a flexible heart, one married to the ultimate good of all concerned. This means that one must hold in one's heart the incredible paradox of one's own truth as well as the truth perceived by others. This is a tension-filled but ultimately creative undertaking that burns away our little, carefully bounded selves.

If we are to have hearts like this we must learn to live with the kind of searing paradox that burns off our narrow preconceptions, our petty self-protectiveness, and our need to control. We must be burned hollow enough to allow that divine expansion to communicate itself to us, to move freely and fluidly between us, to make us passageways through which the Spirit flows.

The third aspect of Sacred Heart devotion that recommends itself richly to me is the insight, perhaps most fully developed in Salesian spirituality, that God's heart is gentle and humble. The Salesian tradition seized upon the scriptural passage found in Matthew 11, in which Jesus invites his hearers to take his yoke upon their shoulders. "Come to me, and learn from me, for I am gentle and humble of heart," he says. As we saw, Francis de Sales took the invitation seriously and made this the core not only of his Christology but also of his spiritual vision.

Since the heart is the source of all our actions, as the heart is, so are they. When the Divine Spouse invites the soul, he says, "Put me as a seal on your heart, as a seal on your arm." Yes, for whoever has Jesus Christ in his heart will soon have him in all his outward ways. For this reason . . . I have wished above all else for you to engrave and inscribe on your heart this holy and sacred motto, "Live Jesus!" . . . With St. Paul, you can say these holy words, "It is no longer I that live but Christ lives in me." In short, whoever wins a person's heart has won the whole person.[74]

To let Jesus live, his gentle humble heart must become one's own. Such a heart is not weak but infinitely strong, because it has the power to disarm and transform all that comes into it. In a letter to her sisters in religion, Jane de Chantal, as mother superior of the Visitation Order, wrote:

As for gentleness of heart, my dear daughters, this is a heart which does not resist anything, is not angry at anything done to it, that bears all, endures all, that is compassionate and full of affection for its neighbor and that does not have any bitterness in it. No, I am not talking about a heart of flesh but a heart [united with God's will and] of the superior part of the soul. Therefore contradictions, persecutions, obstacles and difficulties which come to the truly gentle heart are immediately weakened as soon as they approach it.[75]

Gentleness disarms, that is the sense of Jane's insight. There is nothing passive about true gentleness. It is intensely active. Gentleness wishes no harm to the other; rather, it wishes only and elicits only the good. Nor does gentleness have anything weak in it. Like a young sapling that bends in a storm while a mighty oak snaps and breaks, gentleness exercises flexibility and good humor to negotiate all difficulties.

I think of the techniques of nonviolent resistance that King advocated in his civil rights work, techniques that he had learned from Mahatma Gandhi and Thoreau. He advocated the use of tactics, gestures, and words that could transform a conflict situation by disarming it. Rather than responding as victims or as adversaries and thus further polarizing a conflict, nonviolent resisters were taught to disarm their opponents through unexpected responses that invited the enemy to see them as having common interests or concerns. A situation could be reframed, creatively reinvented, or broken open by disarmed hearts employing the tactics that disarm. Hearts that allow the gentle, humble Jesus to live in them contain the transformative power of God's own gentle love, a love that conquers all and is stronger than death.

A final dimension of Sacred Heart devotion that seems to me to lend itself well to dialogue with nonviolent theory is the idea that the heart is a place of creative suffering. The full-fledged liturgical cult of the Sacred Heart grew out of the more diffuse but widespread devotion to the wounds of Christ, this focused practice being part of the spiritual emphasis of Western Christendom that emphasized the human experience of Jesus and was especially attentive to his passion. William of St. Thierry (1085-1148) is representative, indeed formative, in this devotion to Christ's wounds:

> The treasures of your glory, Lord, were hidden in your heaven. But when your Son, our Lord, and Redeemer was hanging on the cross, the soldier opened his side with the spear and the sacraments of our salvation poured out as blood and water. Now we do not only place the finger of our hand in his side like Thomas did. We enter through the open gate, all the way into the shrine of your soul where all the fullness of God dwells, and all our comfort and salvation. Lord, open the gates of the ark and let your chosen ones enter. Open the door of Your body that all who desire the Secrets of the Son can enter. And let them drink of your hidden wellsprings and let them taste the price of redemption.[76]

Although many of us in the twenty-first century find ourselves perplexed and troubled by the emphasis on suffering within the spiritual tradition, it nevertheless is a powerful and persistent theme. I would caution that the theme of suffering for the sake of Christ, if it is used to rationalize oppression or justify the abuse of others, could simply be disguised violence. But we have access to a long and profound heritage that, taking its cue from the cross, sees suffering incurred on behalf of the kingdom as redemptive. Much of Sacred Heart devotion falls into that category. Perhaps Margaret Mary Alacoque is the most obvious and notable exponent of this dimension of the heart tradition.[77] In a revelation she received some time before her "great revelations" of the Sacred Heart, Margaret Mary was approached by Jesus:

> Jesus showed her a cross covered with flowers. Behold, the bed of my chaste spouses on which I shall make thee consummate the delights of my love. One by one these flowers will fade and nothing will remain but the thorns they now hide from your weakness. But you will feel their points so keenly that all the strength of your love will be needed to accomplish your martyrdom.[78]

The Visitation tradition already carried in it the idea of the martyrdom of love, an idea implicit in all Christian spirituality and given further articulation by Jane de Chantal. But Margaret Mary lived it out with great vividness.[79] Behind her sometimes troubling accounts of her sufferings is the idea that in her own body she continued the redemptive work of Jesus. Her suffering is ultimately transformative not simply imitative. New life, healing, transfiguration, and resurrection spring forth from the deep and consecrated suffering that she experiences. Margaret Mary thus is an example of what was known in pre–Vatican II Catholicism as a "victim soul," individuals chosen by God to so conform themselves to the crucified Jesus that, like him, they become victims of expiation for the sins of the world.

It is only on the level of mystic participation in which our seemingly separate bodies are known to be intimately intertwined that this participatory suffering makes sense. One of the crucial aspects of nonviolent theory is the willingness to take on suffering oneself rather than inflict harm on another. This too is transformative suffering embraced for a vision—the beloved community—larger than oneself and giving ultimate meaning to one's little life. Translated into the idiom of nonviolent theory, the idea of reparation changes from a potentially negative, world-shunning devotional exercise into a passionate and positive practice engaged in out of love for the world.

The tradition of Sacred Heart devotion gives us access to some of the richest and most insightful dimensions of Christian spirituality and theology. The many themes discovered there—the heart is embodied in the particular, the heart is the center where paradoxes are held in tension, the heart is gentle and humble, and the heart is a place of creative suffering—seem to me to lend themselves to a rich dialogue with modern theories of nonviolence and challenge us to open ourselves to the grace to ask for an exchange so that our hearts might become forges of loving transformation in the midst of a violent world.

    disarm then,
      gentle heart,
  whatever with force into your field flies.

Politics of the Heart

"The Church of the National Vow"
Basilique du Sacré Coeur, Paris

"Oh, very adorable and most lovable Heart of Jesus, temple of the most holy and adorable Trinity, furnace of love, ocean of bounty, closet of delights, inexhaustible fountain of all graces, it is from You that we wish to imbibe the waters of true contrition for not having loved You enough and for any offense. Moreover, we choose You for our refuge, our asylum, and all our hope. All in general and each in particular, we take You for our powerful reformer. Oh my divine Savior, give us humble hearts, docile to Your grace, contrite, and humble: we pray You by the excess of Your divine mercy. Enclose us in Your divine Heart and hold us there safe against the rage of our enemies visible and invisible, and deliver us from our pride and our self-love and give us hearts truly charitable, so that at last we may begin under the protection of Your divine Heart a cycle of fervor, humility, and precision in all our holy observance. We beg You this grace, O divine Jesus, for the love of Your Sacred Heart, by that of Your holy Mother, of our holy founders, that You may always find among the nuns of our monastery true worshipers, victims, and slaves prepared to obey You. It is to obtain this favor that we offer You a dozen greetings a year and put ourselves in this paper that we have all signed under the feet of the sun (monstrance) where You are enclosed in the adorable Eucharist, having the intention [in] all our communions to renew this same prayer and make honorable amends to Your divine Heart for ourselves and all sinners. Praised and absorbed be the Heart of Jesus in the Holy Sacrament of the altar. Amen.[80]

—Chronicle of the Visitation of Nantes, eighteenth century

The political tale of France and the heart of Christ is a cautionary tale worth telling, at least briefly.[81] Religious symbols, of course, never function in a vacuum. They are shaped by human culture and, as they mature, they take on new shapes according to the societal matrix in which they are embedded. One of the most daunting tasks of any religious tradition is to attend to the evolving lives of its focal symbols to ensure that in the transition the symbols continue to communicate their core meanings and still "translate" themselves meaningfully into the new context. The seemingly eternal and fractious religious controversies that plague the planet often originate in this very difficult and contested task.

The translation of the Sacred Heart symbol in France over the course of two centuries is a vivid example of this religious and cultural task played out on the stage of French history. It began in earnest with Margaret Mary's visions and her unanswered and perhaps unreceived vision-induced message for Louis XIV to engrave the emblem of the Sacred Heart on his standard, his arms, his heart, and the heart of the court. In return for this consecration he was promised victory over his enemies; the king and the Sacred Heart were to be allies in a world divided by heresy and political conflict. Louis had in fact made religious uniformity a platform of his political hegemony. In 1675 he had revoked the Edict of Nantes, which had allowed French Protestants legal protection in the realm. Under Louis, both royal and religious absolutism would reign.

The Visitandine's message and the hope that it implied did not die with her in 1690. Forty years later Henri François de Belsunce, bishop of Marseilles, consecrated his city to the Sacred Heart in the belief that such an action would call down divine favor upon his municipality. The calamity that provoked this pious and very public consecration was the arrival of the plague at the port city in 1720. Belsunce was encouraged in his actions by another Visitation nun, Anne-Madeleine Remuzat, from the convent at Marseilles. Like her visionary predecessor, Anne Madeleine experienced ecstatic union with the heart of Jesus, participated in an exchange of hearts, engraved the name of Jesus on her breast, and even received the stigmata as a sign of her radical identity with the crucified Lord. Hers was an atoning body like his, one that suffered for the sins of the world. Her visions were felt to be a continuing attempt on the part of the Sacred Heart to communicate the as-yet-unfulfilled desire for a royal consecration of France. So Bishop Belsunce, viewing the plague as a metaphor for the spiritual sickness that French society had contracted, engaged in dramatic public penance for societal sin and consecrated first himself then later his entire diocese to the Sacred Heart. The bishop's gestures caught the public Catholic imagination. Decoded, the theological message was that calamities such as the plague are not natural disasters but acts of God prompted by divine dissatisfaction with a sinful community. The source of God's wrath could be deflected through religious repentance and supplication; the community must appeal for relief through the wounded Sacred Heart.

By the end of the eighteenth century the Marseille story had become a motif in devotional guides intended for public use and a spur to the retreating Catholic and royalist forces that battled the formidable momentum of the French Revolution. That violent political upheaval and its long, bloody aftermath profoundly influenced the destiny of the heart symbol. Although reform factions did not originally intend to attack the church—a financial crisis of the monarchy was the initiating impulse—events led to a fierce and vicious civil struggle between two transcendent values: the Roman Catholic God defended by the monarchy and royalist factions, and the French idea of the republic. Martyrs fell on both sides. Revolutionary and counterrevolutionary aims were fought out in the streets, on battlefields, and in literature, philosophy, and the arts. Religion and royal prerogatives were mocked and attacked. Regional histories and loyalties swayed populations to one side or the other. In the midst of the fray word of new visions emanating from an anonymous Visitandine in Nantes circulated. The command from the suffering Savior through her was emphatic: Revive the wavering faith of the French people through devotion to the Sacred Heart.

Mass production of Sacred Heart images began. Convents across France distributed them as safeguards against harm and what loyalists saw as the sacrilegious evil of the revolution. Miracle stories of divine protection abounded. In dozens of spontaneous ways, the Sacred Heart and its attendant devotional practices appeared in response to the national crisis. One fascinating example is recorded in a lengthy letter penned in 1794 by Mother Marie Jeronyme Verot, superior of the Visitation convent at Lyons.[82] The letter chronicles the fate of that threatened and finally disbanded community as its members fled the country and reconstituted themselves in Mantua, Italy. Central to the convent's morale under siege was the practice of First Friday devotion to the Sacred Heart as it had been outlined by Margaret Mary. The sisters were also consoled by having with them (at great risk) the heart of their founder, Francis de Sales, a relic that they believed bestowed patronal protection.

The Sacred Heart functioned outside the convent as well. It became the most identifiable emblem of the counterrevolution. The emergent republic was characterized as a conspiracy formed against altar and throne, and the Sacred Heart as France's salvation and shield. Part of the popularity of the devotion stemmed from the widely held conviction that King Louis XVI, Queen Marie-Antoinette, and their family were committed to the Sacred Heart. Although the legend that the king's household and France itself had been consecrated to the Sacred Heart was unsubstantiated, it would not be difficult to imagine, given the ubiquity of the devotion and the web of political and religious loyalties in which the royal, noble, and ecclesiastical families of France were entangled. The king's confessor, for example, Père Hébert, was an enthusiast and superior general of the Eudists, whose founder John Eudes had advanced and propagated the heart devotion before Margaret Mary.

Nor did the symbol lose its efficacy after the king and his queen were put to death. Indeed, it was the standard under which a series of rebellions were staged and the insignia of the ultra-royalist groups that supported the eventual restoration of the monarchy. It was the focal symbol of myriad attempts to re-Christianize France in the wake of the compromised revolution. It was the chosen patron of new religious orders that sprang up on the scorched soil. In fact, Madeleine Sophie Barat, foundress of the Religious of the Sacred Heart, a community formed to educate and evangelize the elite Catholic womanhood of restorationist France, campaigned for Louis XVIII to recognize publicly the clandestine consecration of France that his martyred brother Louis XVI was said to have enacted. The restoration even had its new visionary: a teenaged Parisian mattress-maker-turned-nun was credited with seeing visions rearticulating the now 150-year-old demands filtered through Margaret Mary—a royal consecration, an edifice, an annual commemoration.

During the "année terrible" of 1870-1871, when Germany invaded and occupied French territory and civil war erupted in Paris, the Sacred Heart resurfaced with a vengeance alongside intense self-accusation and reflection in private and public settings. It emerged on the lapels of young French men who answered the 1860s call to defend the pope and the papal states against encroaching Italian nationhood. Eventually, the impulse toward national consecration took form in plans to construct a grand church dedicated to the Sacred Heart. Although the Basilique du Sacré Coeur on Montmartre, which today is such an identifiable landmark on the Parisian skyline, eventually became the property of the city of Paris, it was planned as the Church of the National Vow, a symbol of the marriage of monarchy and church, a symbol of the Catholic counter-culture's long fought resistance to the realization of the aims of revolutionary and republican France.

The Sacred Heart had matured into a symbol both private and public, religious and political. To "read" it in France on the cusp of the twentieth century was to read not a monovocal image but an epic saga.

The Dimensions of God

"Sacred Heart"
Br. Michael McGrath, O.S.F.S.

Since we have been introduced venerable brethren, to the innermost mystery of the infinite charity of the Word Incarnate by these words of the disciple "whom Jesus loved and who also leaned on His breast at the supper," it seems meet and just, right and availing unto salvation, to pause for a short time in sweet contemplation of the mystery so that enlightened by the light which shines from the Gospel and makes clearer the mystery itself, we also may be able to obtain the realization of the desire of which the Apostle to the Gentiles speaks in writing to the Ephesians. "That Christ may dwell by faith in your hearts, and that being rooted and founded in charity you may be able to comprehend with all the saints what is the breadth, and length and height, and depth; to know also the charity of Christ which surpasses all knowledge, that you may be filled unto the fullness of God.[83]
—Pope Pius XII, *Haurietis Aquas*, 1956

If I Were

If I were quite small,
    the size of a gentle gesture,
    the height of a look of love,
Perhaps I might find the hidden doorway to your heart.

If I were quite spacious,
    probing the limits of thought,
    imagining infinity's end,
Perhaps I might glimpse the spaciousness of your heart.

If I were to step beyond my bounded self,
  recognize myself in others,
  know their hearts as my own,
Perhaps I might emerge into your boundless heart.

If I were to embrace the world's pain,
  present to each beginning life,
  suffering each sad end,
Perhaps I might touch the wounds etched in your heart.

If I were to dream my day's desire,
  beyond present possibility,
  into the haunts of hope,
Perhaps I might desire the desires of your heart.

As closely linked as the Sacred Heart symbol was with the fate of post-revolutionary French Catholicism, it was not to be completely defined in the global arena by European religious and political conflicts.

In 1856 Pope Pius IX extended the Feast of the Sacred Heart to the universal church. In 1889 the status of the feast was officially upgraded, which meant that the Feast of the Sacred Heart, previously allowed in specific local dioceses, was to be celebrated everywhere in the Catholic world on the Friday in the Octave after Corpus Christi (the exact day revealed in Margaret Mary Alacoque's visions and the same day on which it is placed on the contemporary liturgical calendar). In addition, public as well as private devotion to the Sacred Heart was officially encouraged. The specific practices that the Visitandine visionary and her Jesuit sponsors had envisioned were formally inaugurated—Thursday night adoration, communion on First Fridays. The liturgical texts designed for celebration incorporated much of the rich imagery and language that John Eudes had developed for his pastoral work in the interior missions. Theologians went to work to clarify and systematize the theoretical foundations of the practices that now spread rapidly throughout the world. The object and foundation of the devotion as well as its proper act were specified.[84]

Simultaneous with the rapid politicized expansion of the symbol in France during the eighteenth and nineteenth centuries was the rapid expansion of the symbol into other corners of the Catholic world. Confraternities of the Sacred Heart sprang up all over Europe. From Europe, devotion to the Sacred Heart was introduced into New Spain at the height of the baroque era.[85]

Especially in Mexico it enjoyed immense popularity, and iconographical representations flourished. Sometimes the heart alone was colorfully portrayed. Sometimes the heart appeared exteriorly on Christ's breast. The devotion, including the practice of family consecrations, was widely promoted and took root and thus varying forms in Latin American popular Catholicism. These consecrations, which involved the prominent display of the Sacred Heart in the home, recalled the Lord's promises purportedly made to Margaret Mary Alacoque at Paray-le-Monial: "I will bless every dwelling in which an image of my heart shall be exposed."

Among the handful of religious publications to which the limited, mostly immigrant Catholic population in North America had access was a devotional pamphlet entitled *The Pious Guide to Prayer and Devotion*. Copies of the guide were available in several American editions from 1792. This book, intended for the use of laity, contained a section on devotion to the heart of Jesus that located the origins of the devotion in the visions of "a young woman unknown to the world from the Diocese of Autun in the town called Paroi le Monial in the monastery of the Visitation."[86]

A sign of the ubiquity of the devotion in the New World is the fact that when Elizabeth Ann Seton, the young American Episcopalian widow, converted to the Catholic faith and at the inauguration of the nineteenth century founded the Sisters of Charity, one of the first congregations of women religious in the fledgling American nation, she incorporated a daily exercise of devotion to the Sacred Heart into her community rule.

Internationally the heart may not have been the embattled insignia of royalist pretensions that it was in France, but it did fly as a standard over a Roman church that during those centuries saw itself very much the opponent of the emerging modern world. In 1899 Leo XIII consecrated the entire human community to the Sacred Heart of Jesus. This was the same pope who issued the ground-breaking (for social ethics) *Rerum Novarum (Of New Things)*, which opposed the exploitation of laborers and the dehumanizing working conditions spawned by the Industrial Revolution. Leo was also a strong opponent of the modernist movement, a turn-of-the-century theological current within Catholicism that attempted to come to terms with modern intellectual developments such as historical-critical interpretations of the scriptures. While many of the modernist ideas roundly condemned by Leo and other popes who championed the Sacred Heart devotion were incorporated into the Catholic perspective following Vatican II, for Leo the Sacred Heart was a symbol of devotional, theological, and political significance that juxtaposed the unconditional love of God and the essentialist traditions of the Catholic church in opposition to encroachments against human dignity and the historical critical consciousness of modernity.

The consecration Leo XIII made was singular in its magnitude. But the act of consecration itself was not unique. From Margaret Mary's first personal act of formal commitment, acts of consecration and reparation were everywhere introduced along with the devotion. Especially after 1850, groups, congregations, and orders consecrated to the Sacred Heart were established throughout the Catholic world. For many, this was less an act of religio-political resistance than a deeply spiritual and symbolically specified affirmation of the unconditional love of God.

A case in point is the Missionary Sisters of the Sacred Heart, established in 1880 in Italy. Founding mother Frances Xavier Cabrini (1850-1917) was a small dynamo of a woman whose goal in founding the missionary institute was to give tangible expression to the love of the Sacred Heart of Jesus in a needy and pain-filled world. To that end, between 1880 and 1917, she singlehandedly founded sixty-seven missions, including schools, hospitals, orphanages, and child-care centers throughout the world. The return addresses on her collected letters read like a travelogue: Rome, Milan, Codogno, New York, Granada, Nicaragua, New Orleans, Genoa, Buenos Aires, Victoria, London, Paris, Manchester, Bilbao, Malaga, Canary Islands, Rosario, Mercedes, Santos, Denver, Chicago, Seattle, Rio, Cordoba, Turin.

Pope Leo XIII knew Mother Cabrini. In fact, he gave initial approval to her institute, encouraged her to undertake missions to the United States to aid the immigrant Italian population, paid for many of her numerous voyages, and gave her gifts and funds for the operation of her apostolic activities. For both the pope and the foundress, the Sacred Heart was the source and the end of human life. It was Frances Cabrini's personal and profound love of that heart that fueled her indefatigable missionary quest.

Her letters give evidence of the numerous ways in which the heart devotion permeated late nineteenth- and early-twentieth-century Catholic piety. The themes of adoration and reparation are evident. Also evident is the patronage and protection that the Sacred Heart was believed to supply to those whose lives were consecrated. At the time of the Vatican's final approval of the Missionary Sisters in 1907, Mother Cabrini wrote:

> The Sacred Heart has inspired the Holy Father, the cardinals and the cardinal prefect of priests and regulars with such paternal affection that it is simply marvelous. It more than amply repays all the tribulations we have endured. Help me to thank the Sacred Heart for so many benefits.[87]

Not only did Mother Cabrini view the Sacred Heart as blessing her institute in general, but she saw every step along the way as guided by the Sacred Heart's providential love.

After many tribulations in Rio [1908] the Sacred Heart has favored us by making me come across a beautiful seventy acre estate on a hill with waterfalls and a lake, a furnished house, and all for 100 conti.[88]

During the first year of the terrible conflagration of World War I, she wrote to a Parisian daughter in religion from New York:

I thought you were in the midst of the fray and under the bombs, instead I hear that you are there as calm as can be. I am really very happy. Oh, the Heart of Jesus of Montmairte in whom I have the greatest confidence and to whom I entrusted you will defend you and all of Paris, I hope.[89]

The benevolent protection of the Sacred Heart, of course, called for a radical response. A year later, during the same war, she wrote to a Missionary Sister in Italy:

Among your many friends seek an influential person and ask him to see that our houses in Italy are respected. It is your duty to do all in your power but, above all, abandon yourselves to the Sacred Heart of Jesus and He will think of each of you and guard you as the apple of His eye. Naturally it is necessary to be very good and faithful in all things to merit the protection of that Divine Heart who has done so much to draw us to Himself.[90]

Making reparation for the sin of the world went hand in hand with the missionary's benevolent works of charity—the hospitals, schools, and orphanages—that gave tangible expression to the love of the Sacred Heart. Carnival in Rome on the eve of the 1891 Lenten season provoked this urgent message from Mother Cabrini to her charges:

In these days of carnival the world reaches the height of folly by going wild and thinking that everything is lawful, unmindful of the thorns it is placing in the adorable heart of Christ. Yes, my daughters, Jesus is tortured, manhandled, agonizing in excruciating pain. He looks around to see if there is someone to say a kind word, to relieve His oppression. He turns to you in a special manner, the Missionaries of His Sacred Heart, who once offered yourselves as victims of expiation. Now is the time to do your duty O Missionaries! Fulfill it scrupulously by making reparation to the heart to whom you have consecrated yourselves.[91]

I'm not sure that most American Catholics of the twenty-first century would feel an immediate empathy with Frances Cabrini's particular expressions of love for the divine-human heart. Yet we most certainly would applaud her generous gift of self to others and the audaciousness of her vision and accomplishment. The self-assured barter-and-exchange mentality of the triumphalist pre–Vatican II church was sloughed off along with humankind's naivete in the wake of the Holocaust, Hiroshima, Vietnam, and the regional and national genocides of that bloodiest of all centuries, the twentieth.

Yet there is still profound resonance with the breadth and depth of Frances Cabrini's sense of the love of God. That love is concrete, tactile, and embodied both in the iconography of the devotion and in the intensely personal and loving service that the Missionary Sisters performed. They were the hands, the feet, the eyes, the ears, the arms moved by the heart of Christ.

For this reason I kneel before the Father, from whom every family in heaven and on earth is named, that he may grant you in accord with the riches of his glory to be strengthened with power through his Spirit in the inner self, and that Christ may dwell in your hearts through faith; that you, rooted and grounded in love, may have strength to comprehend with all the holy ones what is the breadth and length and height and depth, and to know the love of Christ that surpasses knowledge, so that you may be filled with all the fullness of God.
—Eph 3:14-19, second reading for the Feast of the Sacred Heart,
Cycle B, New American Bible

In the family photo album that my mother keeps in her California home is a photograph of me at the age of four. The photo is mounted on black paper and framed by four white paper triangles that hold the photo in place; all of this highlights the picture's black-and-white palette. Visible in gray tones are the brick steps leading up to our front porch, the white, vine-spattered posts that support the porch's overhang, and, on the porch itself, a charcoal-hued cardboard box turned upside down. From one end, two pale sets of bare toes protrude. From the other, where an arc of cardboard has been cut away, a small, dark head crested with rows of tightly plaited braids emerges. I am playing "Turtle."

It was, I recall vividly, a favorite game. As was a youth-long fanciful, if occasional, preoccupation with imagining myself inhabiting particular spaces. Closets: If I had to live here, where would things go? Climbing trees: This limb will be the dining room, this limb the parlor. This and "Turtle" were in fact the same game. A game of almost sensual attraction. A game of fitting myself and my life into the specific dimensions of a demarcated space. Feeling the tactile texture of the space's outside limits, the possibilities of upward expansion, the ordering and compacting of necessary functioning.

These childhood fascinations have translated themselves into certain adult preferences. For the decorative-arts displays in museums: reconstituted French Louis Quartorze drawing rooms; a model Japanese tea house into which one can enter and walk shoeless upon tatami matting; English gardens with their tunnels of trellised roses and circling paths that let you ambulate through different vegetative worlds, checkerboards of herbs, and spirals of floral displays; the vast vaulted skeletons of Gothic cathedrals and the comforting confines of chapels nestled in the woods. A fascination with experiencing the dimensions of space.

Contemporary British journalist Karen Armstrong has described our modern religious quest as a search for the sacred dimension of life, a life dimension that ultimately eludes definition but prompts us to reverent silence.[92] What we are about as religious persons, she contends, is entering into the dimensions of God. Perhaps that is why the heart tradition so allures me— not that it "captures" God in an image but that it has provided an imaginative doorway, a portal, into which Christians collectively have made timid yet awestruck explorations of the unfathomable and unlimited dimensions of the sacred. Armstrong's proposal is that, despite the fact that the sacred is a dimension beyond the threshold of our cognitive powers, we nevertheless can, and must, cultivate the capacity to become more aware of and transparent to the sacred dimension of life. We engage in various practices in this effort. For Armstrong herself the twin practices of intellectual study of the great texts of the monotheistic traditions and the discipline of conscious compassion serve to cultivate awareness.

What she is talking about, of course, is the spiritual life, framed in her instance less by the historic practices of a discrete tradition than by the gathered wisdom of a lifelong search in varied traditions. But her point remains. The search for the God-dimension of human life or, put another way, for entering into the dimensions of God, is cultivated by our conscious and continual practices. Our worship. Our prayer. Our study. Our acts of mercy and justice. The disciplines that focus our attention. The disciplines that help us get beyond narrow self-preoccupation.

The heart tradition is at one and the same time a product of Christianity's centuries' long search for God's dimensions and the symbolic focus for a variety of practices that help open us to the dimensions of God.

We cannot, of course, measure God. But we can, and do, point to our experience to give us a glimmer of the dimensions of the divine.

We refer first to what Blaise Pascal called the "God-shaped hollow" in our hearts, which only God can fill. The ache. The precious, painful wound. The empty space too often obscured by the thousand preoccupations of our workaday lives. Discovered often only when those preoccupations are ripped away by the swift action of death, accident, illness, or abandonment. The "God-shaped hollow" has, when probed, no boundaries, no borders. Only the sounding of our longings echoing into infinity.

This is the sort of intimation better sung than said. I hear it resonate especially when I sing the words penned in the early nineteenth century by Frederick W. Faber. Faber was a member, along with his more famous contemporary John Newman, of the English Tractarian movement and a fellow convert from the Anglican to the Roman communion. Sent by Newman to found a chapter of the Oratory (a spiritual community of diocesan priests with community outreach), Faber wrote hymn texts to be used in the nightly services and eucharistic processions that formed the core of London Oratorian devotion. Faber's poetry explores the dimensions of God:

> There's a wideness in God's mercy
> Like the wideness of the sea.
> There's a kindness in God's justice
> Which is more than liberty.
> There is plentiful redemption
> In the blood that has been shed;
> There is joy for all the members
> In the sorrows of the head.
>
> For the love of God is broader
> Than the measures of our mind,
> And the heart of the Eternal
> Is most wonderfully kind.
> If our love were but more simple
> We should take him at his word.
> And our lives would be thanksgiving
> For the goodness of our Lord.
>
> Troubled souls, why will you scatter
> Like a crowd of frightened sheep?
> Foolish hearts, why will you wander
> From a love so true and deep?
> There is welcome for the sinner
> And more graces for the good;
> There is mercy with the Savior,
> There is healing in his blood.

Mercy. Love. Kindness. Welcome. These abstract concepts are hardly spatial metaphors but in Faber's poetry they point to a Christian sense of the dimensions of God that have a spatial connotation. God's mercy is wide. Divine love is broad. In fact, wider than that—the sea—which we might deem very, very wide. And broader than our capacity to conceptualize that which is broad. It is as though Faber wants to say, no, to sing (a better medium of communication for such intimations) that there is a space, an unimaginably wide, broad, roomy space into which we enter when we encounter divinity. The sacred dimension, the space we begin to inhabit when we cultivate those enlivening, focusing, clarifying practices, is infinite spaciousness itself.

There is nothing flabby or sentimental about these intimations. Nothing soft or unexacting. For we are asked not only to sing of, to acknowledge such spaciousness at the core of reality, but we are asked to inhabit it. To become spaciousness itself.

Framed by the green tendrils of a morning-glory vine, they are eight. Fragile flowers form a constellation of purple stars against the vegetative sky of the vine. His widow sits tall among them, bathed in the sunlight of a summer Santa Barbara afternoon. Circled about her are the next two generations: their tall Nordic son, who hefts his infant son on an upraised leg and smiles at his young wife, her brown hair a dark bobbing boat among the sea of blond heads; a single, career-woman daughter in a blue-checked sundress at her mother's left who leans toward the picture's center as if to speak to their son-in-law, a handsome young widower who kneels and wraps his arms protectively around his two toddler boys.

Inside this picture greeting card is a printed Christmas sentiment and a handwritten addendum: "Though unseen, Walter and Lisa are present also in this picture—and in our lives each day." I turn the card face up again and the purple-starred vine comes into focus, calling up long-ago memories of the dense thicket of morning-glories that overran the lower yard of my first childhood home.

Not so close at hand, yet within experience's reach, were the grapevines of my childhood. The sunbathed acreage of California's Central Valley. The miles of vineyards that corridored the highways of childhood's family travel. Vistas of low-lying vines spreading their tendrils out in a maze of interconnected shoots.

These grapevines have become the stuff of adulthood's contemplation, in part because the contours of a native landscape are forever impressed on consciousness and in part because the past decades of Christian worship have brought the images of vine and vineyard into focus. Over and over they occur in scripture. The evidence of an agricultural people who prayed their praise and laments through the vistas of their native landscapes and the experience of their lives. Vines were the source of life and prosperity (Gn 9:20). Prayer for family prosperity imagined a wife as a fruitful vine and children as olive shoots (Ps 128:3). Prophetic utterances of doom foretold languishing vineyards and vines with withered leaves (Is 34:4; 24:7). The House of Israel was the Lord's vineyard, the soil from which the divine gardener longed to harvest good fruit.

> You brought a vine out of Egypt;
> to plant it you drove out the nations;
> Before it you cleared the ground;
> it took root and spread through the land.
>
> The mountains were covered with its shadow,
> the cedars of God with its boughs.
> It stretched out its branches to the sea,
> to the Great River it stretched out its shoots. . . .
>
> God of hosts, turn again, we implore,
> Look down from heaven and see.
> Visit this vine and protect it,
> the vine your right hand has planted. (Ps 80:8-11,
>   14-16, *The Psalms: A New Translation* [Grail])

Throughout the Old Testament vineyards are alluded to both literally and metaphorically as precious possessions and sources of wealth and livelihood. The covenanted people were God's own vineyard, the fruitful community planted by the divine hand. It is no surprise then that the New Testament writers took up the images of the vine and the vineyard and wove them into their theological vision. In the synoptic gospels Jesus is shown exploring the mysteries of the kingdom and his own identity through parables that make copious use of vineyard imagery.

> A man planted a vineyard. . . . Then he leased it to tenants. . . . When the time came he sent a servant to collect from them his share of the produce from the vineyard. But they seized the man, thrashed him and sent him away empty-handed. He sent another . . . then another . . . then a number of others. He still had someone left: his beloved son. He sent him to them last of all. . . . They seized him and killed him and threw him out of the vineyard. (Mk 12:1-10, New Jerusalem Bible; cf. Lk 20:9-17)

And in John's gospel Jesus is identified as the full harvest of the vine that is Israel.

> I am the true vine,
> and my father is the vine dresser. . . .
> Make your home in me as I make mine in you. . . .
> I am the vine,
> You are the branches.
> Whoever remains in me, with me in [them],
> bears fruit in plenty. . . .
> I have told you this
> so that my own joy may be in you
> and your joy be complete.
> This is my commandment:
> love one another,
> as I have loved you.
>   (Jn 15:1-12, New Jerusalem Bible)

Tradition continued to explore the vine metaphor. The church, as the heir to the covenanted promises, became the new vineyard, with Christ as the central vine from which all the branches in the vineyard draw life. In the medieval artistic imagination the cross became a lush, flowering vine. From that vine was harvested the saving wine: the blood of the eucharist. Christ's crucified body was depicted in devotional drawings as a winepress from which the eucharistic drink issued. Bearing the cross upon his back, he was shown leaning over a wide vat into which a living stream poured from his wounded side.

Expanding on the scriptural and traditional imagery of the church as God's vineyard, Catherine of Siena dictated *The Dialogue* and set forth a compelling vision of the church as the mystical body of Christ. In it she formulated three petitions, one of which was for mercy for the church. She recorded God's response by telling of the gift of the redemptive blood of Christ and the responsibility that gift imposes. Chapter 22 casts God's illumination in the metaphor of the vineyard.

> You are the workers I have hired for the vineyard of holy Church. When I gave you the light of holy baptism I sent you by my grace to work in the universal body of Christianity. You received your baptism within the mystic body of holy church by the hands of my ministers. . . . They are my workers in the vineyard of your souls. . . .
>
> Each of you has your own vineyard, your soul, in which your free will is the appointed worker during this life. . . . So you have this knife [baptism] for your free will to use while you have time, to uproot the thorns of deadly sin and to plant the virtues. . . .

Indeed, I am the gardener, for all that exists comes from me… I am the gardener, then, who planted the vine of my only begotten Son in the earth of your humanity so that you, the branches, could be joined to the vine and bear fruit. . . .

You then are my workers. You have come from me, the supreme eternal gardener, and I have engrafted you onto the vine by making myself one with you.

Keep in mind that each of you has your own vineyard. But everyone is joined to your neighbors' vineyards without any dividing lines. They are so joined together, in fact, that you cannot do good or evil for yourself without doing the same for your neighbors.

All of you have one common vineyard, the whole Christian assembly, and you are all united in the vineyard of the body of holy Church from which you draw your life. In this vineyard is planted the vine, which is my only begotten Son, into whom you must be engrafted.[93]

It is strange how death does and does not change things. One is keenly aware of the absence of the deceased. Holidays especially tug at the heart. With my doktorvater it was not the typical holidays—those we celebrated with our respective families—but rather October 31. On that day on our respective liturgical calendars I celebrated All Hallow's Eve and my mentor memorialized Luther's Posting of his 95 Theses on the door of Wittenburg Cathedral. We had a yearly joking exchange: When was I going to become a Lutheran? When was he going to join the Roman church?

I turn the sun-drenched Christmas photo over again. The ways I feel his absence are different from the ways those pictured here do: for them, he was husband, father, grandfather. For my own children, he was godfather. But for me he was mentor and friend, one who sensed the God-shaped hollow in my heart and as teacher, dissertation director, and colleague encouraged me to live into the longing that never quite finds its rest. "There's a wideness in God's mercy, like the wideness of the sea. . . . " We sang it so often together— in carpools to the campus in the red Volkswagen beetle, gathered around the baby grand in his Santa Barbara living room. I remember him always when the words resurface. We knew it set to different melodies, but the lyrics were the same. When I sing it, I call up in music the heart of my mentor and friend.

Absence focuses a living relationship more clearly. What remains is not only memory but a living connection that transcends the seemingly impregnable barrier of death. A bond exists now between myself and this fair-haired family gathered by the morning-glory vines. The connection has many layers and is ultimately a mystery. In part, we share a common faith that death is not the final word; we share a hope that in some manner not yet imaginable we, and he and his daughter (lost much too soon), will not be lost to one another forever. In part, we share the years in which our paths crossed a thousand times because we shared them with him. More profoundly, we carry with us the gifts that he gave, the contours of our lives altered by his presence. Even more deeply, we are connected in the way we remain connected to him through the bond of love. This love is neither sentiment nor wishful thinking. Rather, it is a powerful reality in which we participate when we open our hearts to one another and to the source of love.

In *The Dialogue* Catherine of Siena records God as saying we each have our own vineyard, but that we are joined to one another's vineyards without any dividing line. We are both our own separate selves and not at all separated from one another. Sacramentally, we graft ourselves onto the living vine of love in baptism, but a deep and purposeful grafting must be accomplished by continuing acts of love throughout our lives. Those acts create something real yet invisible. Love enacted creates a permanent presence that does not diminish with death, does not disappear with loss, but goes on acting in and through those who remain. Love made tangible between us manifests itself again and again when what is tangible is no more.

Years ago, on a free afternoon during a conference on the California coast just south of the San Francisco bay, my mentor and I took a car ride inland through the northern wine country. Miles of intertwining ripe vines clustered at the foot of the rounded, rolling hillsides. We stopped at a local winery and bought bottles of aged Merlot to bring home to our respective spouses. The day before he had visited his eldest daughter, by then a young wife and mother and a new professor at a Northern California university campus. He glowed when he spoke of her, the unmistakable glow of a parent whose loving interconnection with his child defies logical description. We stood outside in the gathering dusk. To our left, a low wooden building set aside for visitors made us privy to the centuries-old process of pressing grapes for wine.

In the scriptural tradition Christ is the full harvest of the lovingly planted vine that is Israel. He is the vine, we are the branches. We are told to make our home in him as he has in us—divine life grafted onto humanity so that humanity might become grafted onto the divine. We are invited to love one another as we have been loved. Medieval Christians invite us to know ourselves more keenly as thus grafted, as unfenced vineyards, our lives entwined with neighbor, each vineyard fed and nourished by the other. Through the artistic tradition we are shown Christ as a vine, the intertwining tendrils of life climbing up the wooden trellis of the cross. He is the winepress, the wine of love pouring from his heart in a flow of mercy as wide as the wideness of the sea.

I turn the sunlit group pictured before the morning-glory vines over once again to reveal the handwritten addendum adjacent to the Christmas greeting. "Though unseen, Walter and Lisa are present also in this picture—and in our lives each day."

Shepherd

Georgetown Visitation Cloister
garden
view from the crypt
Photo: Charles Rumph

So to them he addressed this parable. What man among you having a hundred sheep and losing one of them would not leave the ninety-nine in the desert and go after the lost one until he finds it? And when he does find it, he sets it on his shoulders with great joy and, upon his arrival home, he calls together his friends and neighbors and says to them, "Rejoice with me because I have found my lost sheep." I tell you, in the same way, there will be more joy in heaven over one sinner who repents than over ninety-nine righteous people who have no need of repentance.

—Luke 15:3-7, gospel reading
for the Feast of the Sacred Heart,
Cycle C, New American Bible

It is difficult to say at what point the imagery of the Good Shepherd was incorporated into the tradition of the heart. There are fleeting but oblique references to it in Gertrude the Great's effusive poetic ruminations in the thirteenth century. We do not, however, find it explored four centuries later in John Eudes's many hymns, prayers, salutations, litanies, offices, and masses composed in honor of the Sacred Heart. Gentleness and humility are for him attributes of that heart, and images of unbounded ardor, fire, flame, furnace, and majestic love dominate his texts. Certainly Margaret Mary Alacoque's formulations do not include this appellation.

It does, however, appear briefly in the writing of Alphonsus de Liguori (1696-1787), Neopolitan founder of the Redemptorist Order. The bulk of Liguori's prodigious literary output was confined to his mature years, after he had spent decades as a missioner among ordinary people mainly in rural areas. His spiritual doctrine was thus born from his practical and pastoral experience. His aim was, quite simply, to awaken all people, whatever their state of life, to the love of God. Thus he emphasized God's love for humankind. Devotion to the heart of the loving redeemer was central to his pastoral practice. In his "Novena to the Sacred Heart," Liguori outlined a nine-day process of prayer in which the devout person was to meditate on the qualities of the heart of Jesus, which he names as deserving of our love, loving, longing to be loved by us, sorrowful, compassionate, generous, grateful, despised, and faithful. In meditation number five on the compassionate heart of Jesus, Liguori employed the figure of the Good Shepherd along with the figure of the father of the prodigal son, both images of divine compassion for the lost.

> Where could we find a more compassionate and loving heart than the heart of Jesus who has shown such compassion for our miseries? This love made him come down from heaven to earth, made him declare that he is that Good Shepherd ready to lay down his life for his sheep. In order to obtain for us the pardon of our sins, he did not pardon himself but willed to sacrifice himself on the Cross to satisfy, with his sufferings, what we deserved for our sins. This mercy and compassion made him say even to us: "Why should you die, O house of Israel? For I have no pleasure in the death of anyone who dies" (Ez 18:31-32). My poor children, he seems to say, why do you wish to destroy yourselves by fleeing from me? Do you not realize that by fleeing from me you are in danger of eternal death? I have no desire to see you lost; do not delay, turn to me when you will and find your life once more. His compassion leads him to declare that he is that loving father who, even though he sees himself despised by his son, does not reject him when he returns penitent but rather embraces him tenderly and does not remember all the insults he has received.[94]

Exactly contemporary with Liguori, yet on the opposite side of the confessional divide, was baroque composer George Frederick Handel (1685-1757). Perhaps coincidentally (yet it is hard to imagine coincidence in this case), in his great Christmas oratorio, *Messiah*, Handel musically and textually aligned the image of the Good Shepherd with the image of the Matthean Jesus, who is gentle and humble of heart. In this he anticipated modern Roman Catholic liturgical practice. Deep in the drama of the oratorio Handel situated two arias that declare the fulfillment of God's promises in the person of the Messiah. The alto aria is set in the warm, pastoral key of F, with melodic "lines descending like the shepherd stooping to pick up his sheep."[95] The text returns to the same prophetic passage with which the oratorio began.

> He shall feed his flock like a shepherd, and he shall gather the lambs with his arm; and carry them in his bosom, and gently lead those that are with young. (Is 40:11, modified)

The divine promises foreshadowed by the prophet hover over the waiting world. Then the alto's melody is modulated to the higher, brighter key of B flat and the prophetic utterance is answered by the liquid phrasing of the soprano soloist, who sings:

> Come unto him all ye that labour, come unto him that are heavy laden, and he will give you rest. Take his yoke upon you, and learn of him, for he is meek and lowly of heart, and ye shall find rest unto your souls. (Mt 11:28-29, modified)

The coming of the one of meek and lowly heart is the fulfillment of the prophecy. The women's voices intermingle these anticipatory and comforting words. He will carry his people on his bosom and lead them gently. He is the Good Shepherd. He, of such a heart, is our promised rest. "His yoke is easy and his burthen light," the chorus repeats in affirmation.

In Cycle C of the contemporary Catholic lectionary, both the first reading from Ezekiel and the gospel text from Luke designated for the Feast of the Sacred Heart present the image of the heart through the image of the Good Shepherd. Charting the liturgical development of the devotion gives some clue to the circumstances that fostered emergence of this Good Shepherd image.[96] The first office and Mass for the feast were celebrated locally in France by John Eudes in 1672. Between that year and 1840 over thirty different mass formularies were composed for the feast. Four formularies received official approval between 1765 and 1970. The third of these, *Miserebitur (He Will Have Pity)*, was published by Pius IX after he extended the feast to the entire Roman church in 1856. It focused on reparation and the wounded heart and reflected the piety inaugurated by Margaret Mary. The fourth mass formulary, *Cogitationes Cordis Eius (The Thoughts of His Heart)*, was composed in 1929 at the request of Pius XI. It was issued in tandem with his 1928 encyclical *Miserentissimus Redemptor*. This formulary also emphasized the love of God manifest in Christ's suffering and stressed the need for human reparation for sin.

Very different was the tone of the 1954 encyclical of Pius XII, *Haurietis Aquas (You Shall Draw Water)*, which drew more upon the scriptural and patristic legacy of the devotion. *Haurietis Aquas* articulated a theology of the devotion that saw the Sacred Heart as the symbol of a threefold love: the divine love of the preexistent Logos, the perfect love of Jesus for God and humankind, and Jesus' natural affections correspondent with that divine-human love. For Pius XII, the heart of Jesus was the window through which we might contemplate the whole mystery of redemption. The human response to this mystery is, in *Haurietis Aquas,* not to make reparation for sin but to open our hearts to share in Christ's life.

The Heart of Christ is the clearest image of this fullness of God embracing all things. By this we mean the fullness of mercy, which is the special characteristic of the New Testament in which "the goodness and kindness of God our Saviour appeared" (Ti. 3:4). "For God did not send His Son into the world in order to judge the world, but that the world might be saved through Him" (Jn. 3:17). . . .

Devotion to the Most Sacred Heart of Jesus is essentially devotion to the love with which God loved us through Jesus and is at the same time an enlivening of our love for God and man. Or, to put it in other words, this devotion is directed to God's love for us in order to adore Him, thank Him and to spend our lives imitating Him.

It seeks to lead us, in attaining this goal, to a strengthening of the bonds of love, with which we are bound to God and our fellow men, by daily observing more eagerly the new commandment which the Divine Master gave to His disciples as a sacred inheritance when He said: "A new commandment I give you, that you love one another: that as I have loved you, you also love one another. . . . This is My commandment, that you love one another as I have loved you" (Jn. 13:34; 15:12).[97]

The shift in emphasis in this mid-twentieth-century encyclical was mirrored in the liturgical reforms after Vatican II when the Mass and offices for the Feast of the Sacred Heart were revised. The relationship between divine and human love and the mediating heart of Jesus thus received three distinct expressions in the three years of the contemporary liturgical cycle. Focus is alternately upon the covenant relationship with God (Cycle A), the love of God that reconciles us in Christ (Cycle B), and Christ the Good Shepherd (Cycle C), who searches out lost sheep.

For thus says the Lord God: I myself will look after and tend the sheep. As a shepherd tends his flock when he finds himself among his scattered sheep, so will I tend my sheep. I will rescue them from every place where they were scattered when it was cloudy and dark. I will lead them out from among the peoples and gather them from the foreign lands; I will bring them back to their own country and pasture them upon the mountains of Israel [in the land's ravines and all its inhabited places]. In good pastures I will pasture them, and on the mountain heights of Israel shall be their grazing ground. There they shall lie down on good grazing ground, and in rich pastures shall they be pastured on the mountains of Israel. I myself will pasture my sheep; I myself will give them rest, says the Lord God. The lost I will seek out, the strayed I will bring back, the injured I will bind

up, the sick I will heal [but the sleek and the strong I will destroy], shepherding
them rightly.

—Ezekiel 34:11-16, Cycle C, first reading for the Feast
of the Sacred Heart, Jerusalem Bible

In sensate memory I associate the sanctuary with the balmy warmth and horizontal shafts of sunlight so typical of a Southern California afternoon in early fall. I must have been drawn there, on and off, over a period of months, for memory also retrieves images of the tennis courts of Griffith Park and the soft percussion of balls lobbed during lessons as well as of a stack of college textbooks placed pew-side in an autumn ray of sunshine.

It was 1971 or 1972, and the church had been drawing me during the late afternoons. Always weekdays. If I headed homeward from the south or east, I would pass St. Francis Catholic, a structure of 1950s vintage with blond wood pews, a monumental bas-relief of St. Francis of Assisi in graded shades of brown and beige behind the altar, and two wondrous rows of rectangular stained-glass windows refracting the sunlight into rainbow ribbons that undulated slowly over the length of the sanctuary as the afternoon waned.

At the time I was not a Catholic, although I had been joined in matrimony just a few years before in a Catholic church across town because my young husband was, at least nominally, part of that communion. Vatican II's reforms had not yet been instituted at Christ the King, and I had alternately wept and gnashed my teeth through a Pre-Cana booklet that outlined the essentials of the Roman faith and had agreed, as the unchurched outsider, to raise the offspring of this union within the Roman fold. While I struggled mightily with what seemed like ludicrous views on unbaptized infants and teachings on the proper use of sacred implements and articles, I was compelled by the realization of a worldwide community. My husband-to-be, of pallid belief and minimalist practice, could go anywhere on the globe, walk into a Catholic church, and find himself utterly at home. So I sat stoically through the sessions in the green booklet, and I signed the prenuptial agreements. But I had not joined.

The year I began stopping by St. Francis on my way home I was (although I did not know it then) halfway into what would be a six-year marriage and barely a year into a returning student's bachelor of arts degree in history. I was lured by the silence of the empty space, lured into a sacred enclosure that, in an instant, placed me in an atmosphere so stunningly distinct from the jarring, exhaust-clogged streets I had just traversed. It took my breath away.

What first drew me inside remains obscure, but the cumulative sense of the place remains vivid, even after thirty years. When the fall quarter commenced, I began to bring my school books with me: a study of feudalism, the

Life of Charlemagne by Nottger the Stammerer, Panofsky's classic *Gothic Art and Scholasticism*. The primary sources for a course in Western European history. These books, stacked on the pew or opened on my lap, found a resonant echo in the images on the stained glass surrounding me. St. Louis was not only the mythic holy figure whose translucent red robes were outlined in lead, he was the political leader of the emergent French monarchy.

I brought my books and sometimes searched for clues to the identities of others of those stained-glass saints. But more often than not the books remained in their stacks or unopened on my lap, and I simply sat in the undulating ribbons of colored light that passed slowly by and over me, breathing in the scent of honeysuckle as it drifted in from outside and blended with the lingering odors of incense and warmed candle wax. It felt like coming home.

Then one day, quite unexpectedly, everything changed. I must have been frequenting St. Francis for months, for I remember anticipating the familiar serenity of my late afternoon idyll. I was sitting halfway back in the church in the left bank of pews and had my eyes directed toward the oversized bas-relief Francis, who solicitously bent over to feed a flock of eager birds gathered at the hem of his robes. Everything was in soft focus, my focused attention suspended, as is often the case when one enters a quasi-meditative state.

Suddenly I was jolted into awareness. I want to say that I *saw* this, but there was nothing material about the seeing. It came as an insight, an insight with the absolute clarity and authority of physical sight. First, I experienced viscerally that God was the single, most central fact and desire of my life. As urgent as breath. The sensation was of being swept into a vortex of irresistible force only to find myself at a silent center. Here was a pure point into which all my intellectual, emotional, spiritual, physical, and volitional energies had been drawn, leaving them pulled taut, well beyond their usual boundaries. The insight shuddered through me, leaving in its wake waves of longing.

In the same instant I saw clearly that my life, as presently lived, was out on the periphery, light years away from this silent center. The realization cannot be described as a "conviction" of sin: particular acts or habits did not present themselves for unveiling. Rather, I experienced an incredible force sweeping my energies back toward their accustomed places, far away from this silent center.

I knew that I must be at this center or cease to be. I knew as well that I was incapable of remaining there. I knew these two terrible things at one and the same time. Then, from some unimagined reserve, I summoned a prayer from that silent space before the fragmenting force swept me away. The prayer lasted only a moment and had no content except these simultaneous knowings: I must. I cannot.

Then I rose and, quitting the rainbow-flecked sanctuary, went out into the fading light. The gathered energies dispersed. I was losing myself, leaving only the echo of that wordless prayer flung into the dark.

How dark the seeing. How fragmentary. Mostly it consists of learning to free fall. Learning to trust the constant somersaulting. Learning to live with spiritual vertigo. Learning to love the darkness. Learning to trust the brief glimpses. Learning that blindness is its own seeing. Learning that the falling is in itself beautiful. That at the bottom of the well of my heart, I free fall into You.

The Center and End of All

Sacred Heart Icon
Robert Lentz

The great secret, the great mystery, is this: there is a heart of the world . . . and this heart is the heart of Christ.[98]

—Pierre Teilhard de Chardin,
1881-1955

Two towering twentieth-century theologians—both priests of the Jesuit order—made the Sacred Heart a source for theological reflection. Karl Rahner and Pierre Teilhard de Chardin both came from devout Catholic families where Sacred Heart devotion was the warp and woof of religious identity. And both

Heart of Matter

Blessed be you,
  heart of matter, hand of God, heart of God.
Blessed be you, harsh matter,
  barren soil, stubborn rock.
Blessed be you, perilous matter,
  violent sea, untamable passion.
Blessed be you, mighty matter,
  March of evolution, the always, ever new.
Blessed be you, powerful matter,
  in whom the multitude of monads are
    bound.
Blessed be you, mortal matter, dying
  you lead to the heart of all that exists.

You batter us and dress our wounds,
You resist then yield to us,
You wreck and build,
Shackle and liberate,
You sap of our souls.

Hand of God,
Flesh of Christ,
You I bless.
You I bless.

In your oceans stirs the Spirit;
In your fountains, our soul's source.
In your clay slumbers the incarnate Word.
At your molten core seethes the heart of God.

Raise me up, sweet matter.
Take me in your arms,
Where flesh is so transparent
It is the memberance of infinity.

Raise me up, fierce matter.
Let the universe's embrace melt me,
Melt me
In the fiery heart of God.[99]

110

were formed as young priests by the devotion as it was encouraged by the Society of Jesus. Neither of these theological giants is remembered primarily today as one who explicitly promoted the devotion, although Rahner, among the multitude of topics he considered, did apply his prodigious intellect to a reinterpretation of the theology of the devotion.[100]

Rahner's reconsideration of the devotion as it was popularly practiced in the Pre–Vatican II church retrieved its biblical basis and refocused the devotion away from its sentimental and sin-conscious Paray-initiated form to place it in the mainstream of modern theology. Hence he criticized the emphasis on reparation, asserting that only Jesus Christ can make true reparation. He claimed that a Christian only *participates* in the reparation Jesus has made on the cross. Likewise, Rahner affirmed that Jesus no longer suffers in his glorified humanity; reparation and the sense of Jesus presently crucified by the world, which had become so prevalent, were critiqued.

Instead, Rahner saw the heart of Jesus as a "primordial word" that defies definition and points to the mystery of God. It points to the unity of divinity and humanity, of spirit and flesh. Beyond this, Rahner understood the word *heart*, in the biblical sense, as signifying the center of the whole person, not merely as the seat of the affections. Thus the heart of Christ is a symbol of the whole person of Christ and manifests his salvific reality. The heart of Christ reveals the center of the Savior who mediates God's grace, forgiveness, and intimacy to humankind. It is a heart both human and divine. The human heart of Jesus is the place of his free surrender to the mystery of God, even to death. The heart is also the heart of the risen Christ. For Rahner, the resurrection was God's acceptance of the Savior's free surrender. As the heart is the center of humanity's personal freedom and surrender to God, so the Sacred Heart is the center of Christ's freedom and surrender. This heart freely chose to be pierced by sin and freely given in the eucharist as the source of our love for one another.

Rahner predicted that the devotion would change in the wake of Vatican II. He believed that a few people would choose to draw strength from the pierced Heart of Christ in order to live for others with compassion. Love of neighbor, in his view, would become a contemporary form of Sacred Heart devotion. The concrete love of others, which has both social and political implications, could sustain itself for love by entering into the attitudes and dispositions of the heart of Jesus Christ.

Just as Karl Rahner's Sacred Heart was a center of the twin actions of love of God and neighbor, so it was a center for Rahner's slightly older contemporary, Pierre Teilhard de Chardin.[101] Unlike Rahner, who was an academic, Teilhard was a scientist by profession. A paleontologist to be exact. At the core of his utterly unique and extraordinary spiritual-theological vision was the Sacred Heart of his childhood. Like Rahner, he was critical of the popular Paray form of the devotion, finding it wanting in its obsession with sin and its sentimentality. Instead, over a lifetime of reflection the Sacred Heart took on the quality of a cosmic fire for Teilhard. He experienced the symbol as mediating the two conflicting directions of humankind in the twentieth century— the upward movement toward the infinite and the forward march of evolution. (One can see the priest and the scientist struggling here.) In Christ's heart, Teilhard believed, both detachment and progress, prayer and action, love for God and love for the world are reconciled.

The progress of Teilhard's spiritual vision focused on the Sacred Heart can be mapped at crucial points in his life. In 1916 he wrote of Jesus' heart as filling the world with the power of Christ's love and in a poetic essay described the mystical vision of "a friend" (a subterfuge for himself) who, contemplating a picture of the Sacred Heart, experienced the outlines of the figure dissolve and the vibrant power of Love fill the world. This was the first flowering of the symbol for Teilhard. What would eventually blossom would be one of the most extraordinary of Christian mystical visions. The Sacred Heart would become not only the love of Jesus for humankind but also the unifying meaning and force of that love as it unites and gives meaning to all human hope.

By 1939 Teilhard was experiencing the heart of Jesus risen as the Omega-point, the future point of all evolution's convergence. By 1940 he explained how his concept of the universal, cosmic Christ was "born from an expansion of the heart of Jesus." By the 1950s he made reference to "the heart of the Heart of the World, the center of the Center of the Universe." By the end of his life, he was able to pray in his personal yearly retreat of his union with Jesus in terms of his reinterpreted devotion to the Sacred Heart.[102]

What personally drove Teilhard's cosmic vision was the need to adore the Absolute through what is tangible. The theological and scientific worlds in which he was trained cried out for synthesis and concrete thought. In the heart of Christ he discovered the materialization of God's love—at one and the same time spiritual, tangible, and energizing.

> Under the symbol of the Sacred Heart, the divine assumed for me, the form, the strength and the properties of an energy, of a fire. . . . Through its power to become universal, this fire proved able to invade and impregnate with love the whole atmosphere of the world in which I lived.[103]

The heart enabled Teilhard to bring into single focus both his attraction for matter and his adoration of the Person of Christ. It summarized both the forward thrust of evolution and the upward yearning of transcendent life.

This passionate cosmic vision put Christ at the center of the universe—as the reality that binds together into a unity the totality of creation. Hence the cosmos was Christic. And all its evolutionary drives converged at the eschatological endpoint. This Omega-point was none other than the human heart of the risen Christ. Thus, Teilhard could write in his essay "Cosmic Life," the following prayer:

> Lord Jesus Christ, you truly contain within your gentleness, within your humanity, all the unyielding immensity and grandeur of the world. And it is because of this, it is because there exists in you this ineffable synthesis of what our human thought and experience would never have dared join together in order to adore them—element and totality, the one and the many, mind and matter, the infinite and the personal; it is because of the indefinable contours which this complexity gives to your appearance and to your activity, that my heart, enamoured of cosmic reality, gives itself passionately to you.
>
> I love you, Lord Jesus, because of the multitude who shelter within you and whom, if one clings closely to you, one can hear with all the other beings murmuring, praying, weeping. . . .
>
> I love you because of the transcendent and inexorable fixity of your purposes, which causes your sweet friendship to be coloured by an intransigent determinism and to gather us all ruthlessly into the folds of its will.
>
> I love you as the source, the activating and life-giving ambience, the term and consummation, of the world, even of the natural world, and of its process of becoming.
>
> You the center at which all things meet and which stretches out over all things so as to draw them back into itself: I love you for the extensions of your body and soul to the farthest corners of creation through grace, through life, and through matter.
>
> Lord Jesus, you who are as gentle as the human heart, as fiery as the forces of nature, as intimate as life itself, you in whom I can melt away and with whom I must have mastery and freedom: I love you as a world, as this world which has captivated my heart; and it is you, I now realize that my brother-men, even those who do not believe, sense and seek throughout the magic immensities of the cosmos.
>
> Lord Jesus, you are the center towards which all things are moving: if it be possible, make a place for us all in the company of those elect and holy ones whom your love care has liberated one by one from the chaos of our present existence and who now are being slowly incorporated into you in the unity of the new earth.[104]

An ache. Foundations deep in the human heart. Arching out. Pressing past ribs. Knocking the wind from lungs. Prying open the breastbone. Constricting the throat. It thrusts out, splitting open the small vessels that are our lives. Its curve vaults to infinity.

Los Angeles, the late 1960s. A summer afternoon wilted in the dry heat of the sun. I have been apartment hunting, touring the palm-shaded streets adjacent to L.A. City College. Something cheap but with character. I've shied away from the large, modern complexes and kept an eye peeled for those bungalow-lined courts, small stucco units that peer at each other across a rectangle of lawn bordered with bright pansies or geraniums. At just such a one, I stop, drawn by a hand-lettered sign, "One Bedroom for Rent, See Manager Number 4." The property is poorly kept; foxtails threaten to choke out the flowering plants.

At the end of the row of identical cottages, each with its unique pattern of peeling paint, the door to number 4 is open. A cavern inside is inky black in contrast with the fierce sunlight in which I stand. Shielding my face, I peer in and am startled, once my eyes adjust, to find myself in close proximity to a young woman with long, glossy, black hair pulled taut in a low ponytail. She is seated on a shabby overstuffed sofa; she holds a small child on her lap. The furnishings are few and drab, but the room is filled with the pulsing sound from a phonograph located somewhere out of view.

The Beatles—or perhaps Jefferson Airplane—spin a haunting cocoon of layered sound that envelops the young woman tightly. She is lost in it, light years away from the dim, drear place in which she sits. I have caught her not simply listening to music but in an act equivalent to prayer. She cannot be much older than I am. No doubt she holds the position of on-site manager in exchange for reduced or negligible rent, a necessity brought on by the child on her lap. It is a job that requires her to be at home all day.

The intimacy of the moment is almost unbearable. The extent to which the aching melody transforms the dead-end day, perhaps the dead-end life, of this very young, very trapped woman, is startlingly obvious. It is as though I have unwittingly stepped into some painful, private revelation. A confession, not simply of tedium and isolation, but of the irrepressible ache that vaults up and out from the heart beyond these confining walls, propelled by the music's soaring melodies.

Inscribed

"One Heart, One Soul"
Francis de Sales and Jane de Chantal
Br. Michael McGrath, O.S.F.S.

Certainly, in the Incarnation He has made us see that which otherwise the human mind could hardly have imagined or understood, that is, that God was human and a human being was God: the immortal, mortal; the One incapable of suffering, suffering—subject to heat, cold, hunger and thirst; the infinite, finite; the eternal, temporal—in short, [in Jesus] the human divinized and God humanized in such a way that God, without ceasing to be God, is human; and a human, without ceasing to be human, is God.[105]

—Francis de Sales,
seventeenth century

Dozens of fifty-foot long curtains of artificial lights wink just overhead. Suspended from the steel-girded beams that form the frame of the monumental conservatory, they cascade downward between the waving fronds of tropical palms and the spray of tumbling waterfalls. It is fading dusk in the ersatz environment of Nashville's Opryland Hotel at the close of the liturgical year, Anno Domini 2000, and the entertainment complex is decorated for the holidays. Dwarf-sized animated figures wave from multicolored hanging hot-air balloons or peer through tropical foliage like fantastic bright rain-forest fowl. In one niche of the maze of arenas, courts, and lobbies is a chalky-white plasticine nativity display—life-sized angelic messengers trumpeting, the holy family making its donkey-straddled way toward a welcoming stable. The air is agitated with the rush of falling water and the recorded strains of "Jingle Bells." It is not yet Thanksgiving.

I am seated on a rattan lawn chair on the simulated equatorial patio outside the Jack Daniel Saloon, waiting for my colleagues who are also attending the annual convention of the American Academy of Religion. I wonder why the academy is at this site this year and consider the fact that three decades ago I fled the Disneyland-like entertainment world to begin a serious study of religion, left the world of illusions and fantasy for the world of mythic imagination. The irony of full-circling! My colleagues arrive to order artichoke dip and chips and thoughtfully ask what I have been doing here this last half hour. "Thinking about the Sacred Heart," I reply. "Explain to me what that's all about," my Protestant scripture-scholar colleague leans back in his rattan cage. "Its so gruesome and incomprehensible, that bodily organ all bathed in blood!" I try to explain by giving a brief history of the image, but my attempt falls short. He remains skeptical. Although I don't, I want to say, "You have to live with it a long time."

My mind is crowded with motifs of all sorts. Each points to the reciprocal love of humanity and the divine: mystical exchange, adoration and reparation, ecstatic outpouring, mutual breathing and beating, feasting and feeding, wounds and clefts, refuge and rest, the breast of the beloved, the bridal bed, sacrifice and pierced flesh, suffering and streams of blood, flames and fiery furnaces, fountains and mystical dew, consecration and patronage, gentleness and shepherding, spaciousness and mercy to infinitude.

One final motif rises to awareness. Jane de Chantal introduced me to it during the years of writing my dissertation. Despite her extended family's insistence, the young seventeenth-century widow had determined that she would not remarry but rather give herself wholly to God. Her marriage to the handsome Baron de Chantal had been a happy one and produced four children. But in her grief, Jane discerned a different life itinerary. She put herself under the spiritual direction of Francis de Sales, the popular preacher and bishop from Savoy, and launched into the spiritual life with characteristic ardor. Praying before a delicate carved wooden crucifix, she took up a heated implement and branded the name of Jesus on the flesh above her heart. Her director was not pleased, for his preferred methods of formation were less literal. Instead, he urged her to focus on the practices of prayer and charity that would produce an interior engraving of her heart.

The motif of inscribing the name of Jesus on the heart was not new in the seventeenth century. When Bishop de Sales, in his *Introduction to the Devout Life* alluded to the practice in its metaphorical form, by comparing the human heart to the seed of an almond tree (which when carved upon and planted, produces a tree with almonds bearing identical carvings), he was picking up an ancient Christian motif. (He was also following the classical naturalist Pliny in his odd botanical assertions.) The point for de Sales was that "whoever has Jesus Christ in his heart will soon have him in all his outward ways."[106]

The motif of the engraved or inscribed heart harkened back to both medieval romance—a lover's heart in lyrics often spelled the name of his beloved—and lives of the saints.[107] Notable among the saints with hearts inscribed were Ignatius of Antioch (d. 107) and Henry Suso (d. 1366). Medieval hagiography represented Ignatius as repeatedly invoking the name of Jesus in the presence of his executioners, compelled by the fact that that name was written on his heart. One legendary tradition had the martyred Ignatius's heart cut open to be read and divided to provide relics. The gold letters forming the divine name were said to be found written on each individual piece. More literal, and apropos of Jane de Chantal's ardent gesture, was Dominican Henry Suso, who took a stylus to his own flesh and engraved the letters IHS (Jesus Christ) over his left breast. Suso's female devotees embroidered these letters in red silk on small strips of cloth and took to wearing them pinned to their own breasts.

In more metaphorical manner, the early modern era, of which de Sales's sensibilities were an example, took up the idea of the inscribed heart. Christ-like virtues were cultivated. The proclamation "Live Jesus," the motto of the Visitation taken up by others, like John Eudes, translated the inscription theme. We still hear echoes of the theme today in churches across the English-speaking world when we sing the last stanza of the familiar hymn penned by Charles Wesley.

> Your nature gracious Lord, impart,
> come quickly from above,
> Write your new name upon my heart,
> Your new best name of love.[108]

The loving human heart is to be marked with the name of the beloved, claimed and won.

And what of the divine heart? A hint is found once again in the Salesian tradition. In a remarkable Lenten sermon delivered in what was to be the last year of his life, Bishop de Sales offered a vision of heaven to the Visitation nuns who were his listeners. His vision was profoundly relational—eternal beatitude was imagined as reunion with those loved in life as well as loving converse with the saints and the members of the Trinity. In an astonishing passage Francis imagined the encounter with the Second Person. In a gesture of loving intimacy, God-become-flesh privileged the blessed with knowledge of his heart and of the reciprocal love that burns there.

> Let us pass on, I pray you, and say a few words about the honor and grace that we will have in conversing even with our incarnate Lord. Here, undoubtedly, our felicity will reach in inexpressible and unutterable height. What will we do, dear souls, what will we become, I ask you, when through the Sacred Wound of His Side we perceive that most adorable and most loving Heart of our Master, aflame with love for us—that Heart where we see each of our names written in letters of

love! "Is it possible, dear Saviour," we will say, "that you have loved me so much that you have engraved my name in Your Heart?" It is indeed true. The Prophet, speaking in the name of Our Lord, says to us: "Even though a mother forget the child she carried in her womb, I will never forget you, for I have engraved your name in the palms of my hands" (Is. 49:15-16). But Jesus Christ, enlarging on these words, will say, "Even if it were possible for a woman to forget her child, yet I will never forget you, since I wear your name engraved on my Heart."[109]

There are a few families with children passing through the hoard of religion scholars intently gathered in pairs disputing the latest hermeneutical conundrums confronting those in their profession. The smallest children race ahead of their parents and shout out when they discover a new Santa's workshop elf or nutcracker soldier hidden among the palms. My youngest and third child is now a lanky sixteen, and the toddler squeals nearby send me back to earlier days—he on hip, his sisters ahead climbing into the swan boats on the Boston Commons or his hand clasped tightly in mine as eager siblings streak ahead to be first in line on Disneyland's Dumbo ride.

My son was born by Caesarian section at Boston's Brigham and Women's Teaching Hospital. Not that it had been planned that way. Recent studies from UCLA had shown no statistical increase of uterine rupture in women with two previous C-sections who delivered vaginally a third time. Most of the data were gathered from among the migrant working population who had had no prenatal care but simply showed up at the hospital far advanced in labor. But the medical residents at Brigham and Women's were convinced by the statistics and urged me to consider a natural delivery. I had hoped for a natural delivery twice before, so I concurred. But things did not go as anticipated, and after a draining, unproductive labor and the lengthy interruption of another woman's surgical emergency in the delivery room, I was operated upon again. But this time was different. After the initial incision the young surgically garbed physician took a sharp breath and spoke quietly to me: "You were lucky. The scar tissue is paper thin. Much longer and you two might not have made it."

For a week the baby and I were sequestered in a quiet room away from the worst of the noisy hospital traffic. A steady rain grayed the late-June Boston sunlight and shrouded our one thin rectangle of window. I grieved the substantive loss of life-giving capacity. "It would not be a good idea to try this again," the medical advisors warned. But I also wondered at the strange mystery of new life stepping so innocently aside from death's shadow. And I marveled at the angry red wound sliced just a hair's breadth below the twin lines of scar tissue already inscribed on the flesh of my belly.

One is never the same. After each birth, the body readjusts. But things are never as they were before. Silver-webbed stretchmarks are only an outward sign. More hidden are the now elastic vessels of the vascular system, the pliancy of muscle walls, the flat pouch of the once inhabited womb. Each child impresses upon waxen flesh the unique imprint of its life. Inscribes one's own life with an image all its own.

Often I have thought how true that is of the heart as well. Each child occupies its own space and in growing presses and pushes out the bounded contours of one's heart. Each fashions a singular, ample habitation like no other. A habitation crowded with an unrepeatable lifetime sorrow and joy. A habitation inscribed with a name. How could it be otherwise in the heart of God?

Appendix

Traditional Litany of the Sacred Heart

Lord, have mercy on us.
  Christ, have mercy on us.
Lord, have mercy on us. Christ, hear us.
  Christ, graciously hear us.
God the Father of Heaven,
  Have mercy on us.
God the Son, Redeemer of the World,
  Have mercy on us.
God the Holy Ghost,
  Have mercy on us.
Holy Trinity, One God,
  Have mercy on us.

Heart of Jesus, Son of the Eternal Father,
  Have mercy on us.
Heart of Jesus, formed by the Holy Ghost in the
    womb of the Virgin Mother,
  Have mercy on us.
Heart of Jesus, substantially united with the Word of
    God, *etc.*,
Heart of Jesus, of infinite majesty,
Heart of Jesus, holy Temple of God,
Heart of Jesus, Tabernacle of the Most High,
Heart of Jesus, House of God and Gate of Heaven,
Heart of Jesus, burning Furnace of charity,
Heart of Jesus, Vessel of justice and love,
Heart of Jesus, full of goodness and love,
Heart of Jesus, Abyss of all virtues,
Heart of Jesus, most worthy of all praise,
Heart of Jesus, King and center of all hearts,
Heart of Jesus, in Whom are all the treasures of
    wisdom and knowledge,
Heart of Jesus, in Whom dwelleth all the fullness of
    the Divinity,
Heart of Jesus, in Whom the Father was well
    pleased,

Heart of Jesus, of Whose fullness we have all
received,
Heart of Jesus, desire of the everlasting hills,
Heart of Jesus, patient and abounding in mercy,
Heart of Jesus, rich unto all who call upon Thee,
Heart of Jesus, Fountain of life and holiness,
Heart of Jesus, Propitiation for our sins,
Heart of Jesus, filled with reproaches,
Heart of Jesus, bruised for our offenses,
Heart of Jesus, made obedient unto death,
Heart of Jesus, pierced with a lance,
Heart of Jesus, Source of all consolation,
Heart of Jesus, our Life and Resurrection,
Heart of Jesus, our Peace and Reconciliation,
Heart of Jesus, Victim for our sins,
Heart of Jesus, Salvation of those who hope in Thee,
Heart of Jesus, Hope of those who die in Thee,
Heart of Jesus, Delight of all the saints,

Lamb of God, Who takest away the sins of the world,
Spare us, O Lord.
Lamb of God, Who takest away the sins of the world,
Graciously hear us, O Lord.
Lamb of God, Who takest away the sins of the world,
Have mercy on us.

Litany of the Heart

Heart of Jesus, hear our prayer

So loving
So humble
So gentle
So compassionate
So faithful
So wise
So patient
So steadfast
So tender
So spacious

Heart of Jesus, hear our prayer

God's joy
God's shalom
Harp of the Trinity
Wingbeat of the Spirit
Breath of God
Five-petaled rose

Heart of Jesus, hear our prayer

Womb of justice
Birthplace of peace
Our dearest hope
Longing of our lives

Heart of Jesus, hear our prayer

Freely flowing fountain
Spring of grace
Freshet of forgiveness
Merciful river
Mystical dew

Heart of Jesus, hear our prayer

Warmth of our hearts
Transforming fire
Cosmic Furnace
Enflamer of hearts

Heart of Jesus, hear our prayer

Heart of evolution
Beginning and ending
Center of all

Heart of Jesus, hear our prayer

Garden of virtues
Mystical dew
Table and food

Heart of Jesus, hear our prayer

Our refuge
Our shelter
Our comfort
Our rest
Our welcoming breast

Heart of Jesus, hear our prayer

Wounded by love
Pierced by our cruelty
Broken by our hardness
Mystic winepress
Poured out as gift

Heart of Jesus, hear our prayer

Have mercy, gracious heart,
Give us gratefulness
Teach us tenderness
Let us learn to love

Hear our prayer.[110]

Promises of the Sacred Heart Given to Margaret Mary Alacoque

1. I will give them all the graces necessary in their state of life.

2. I will give peace in their families and will unite families that are divided.

3. I will console them in all their troubles.

4. I will be their refuge during life and above all in death.

5. I will bestow the blessings of heaven on all their enterprises.

6. Sinners shall find in my heart the source and infinite ocean of mercy.

7. Tepid souls shall become fervent.

8. Fervent souls shall rise quickly to great perfection.

9. I will bless those places wherein the image of my heart shall be exposed and honored and will imprint my love on the hearts of those who would wear this image on their person. I will also destroy in them all disordered movements.

10. I will give to priests who are animated by a tender devotion to my divine heart the gift of touching the most hardened hearts.

11. Those who promote this devotion shall have their names written in my heart, never to be effaced.

12. I promise you in the excessive mercy of my heart that my all-powerful love will grant to all those who communicate on the First Friday in nine consecutive months, the grace of final penitence: they will not die in my disgrace, nor without receiving their sacraments. My divine heart shall be their safe refuge in this last moment.

Notes

1. Cf. A. Vermeersch, S.J., *Practical Devotion to the Sacred Heart* (New York: Benziger Bros., 1909), Joseph McDonnell, S.J., *The Promises of the Sacred Heart* (New York: Benziger Bros., 1913), Charles Santley, *Meditations for Each Day of the Month of June Dedicated to the Sacred Heart of Jesus* (New York: Benziger Bros., 1910), Peter J. Arnoudt, S.J., *The Imitation of the Sacred Heart of Jesus* (New York: Benziger Bros., 1904), Rev. A. Biskupek, S.V.D., *The Litany of the Sacred Heart* (Milwaukee, Wis.: The Bruce Publishing Company, 1956), Alban J. Dachauer, S.J., *The Sacred Heart: A Commentary on* Haurietis Aquas (Milwaukee, Wis.: The Bruce Publishing Co., 1959).

2. Histories of the Sacred Heart are many. Classic among them is Rev. J. V. Bainvel, S.J., *Devotion to the Sacred Heart: The Doctrine and Its History* (London: Burns, Oates and Washbourne, 1924). Helpful modern studies are *Faith in Christ and the Worship of Christ*, ed. Leo Scheffczyk, trans. Graham Harrison (San Francisco: Ignatius Press, 1986); *Heart of the Saviour: A Symposium on Sacred Heart Devotion*, ed. Josef Stierli, trans. Paul Andrews (New York: Herder and Herder, 1958); Timothy O'Donnell, *Heart of the Redeemer* (San Francisco: Ignatius Press, 1989).

3. I take this insight from Michel de Certeau, *The Mystic Fable: The Sixteenth and Seventeenth Century*, trans. Michael B. Smith (Chicago: University of Chicago Press, 1992).

4. On the patristic contribution to the Sacred Heart tradition, see Hugo Rahner, "The Beginnings of the Devotion in Patristic Times," in Stierli, *Heart of the Saviour*, 37-57.

5. On the medieval era, see Josef Stierli, "Devotion to the Sacred Heart from the End of the Patristic Times down to Saint Margaret Mary," in Stierli, *Heart of the Saviour*, 55-108; Walter Baier, "Key Issues in Medieval Sacred Heart Piety," in Scheffczyk, *Faith in Christ and the Worship of Christ*, 81-99.

6. See Josef Stierli, "The Development of the Church's Devotion to the Sacred Heart in Modern Times," in Stierli, *Heart of the Saviour*, 109-130.

7. Inspired by an inscription on the pillars of St. John Lateran by Deacon Leo—later Leo the Great—c. 430. Text: Wendy M. Wright; tune: Kevin Vogt © 2000. Leo's inscription: Virgineo faetu Genitrix Ecclesia natos quos spirante Deo concipit, amne parit. . . . Fons hic est vitae qui totum diluit orbem sumens de Christi vulnere principium. This and all other songs were performed on June 30, 2000 (Feast of the Sacred Heart) at Duchesne Academy of the Sacred Heart, Omaha, Nebraska, for the Bicentennial of the Religious of the Sacred Heart, and on August 5, 2000, at Georgetown Visitation Preparatory School, Washington, D.C., for the Fourteenth Annual Salesian Spirituality Conference.

8. Cyprian (d. 258), *Letters*. Quoted in Stierli, *Heart of the Saviour*, 46-47.

9. Ambrose (c. 339-397), *Expl. of the Psalms*. Quoted in Stierli, *Heart of the Saviour*, 49.

10. Origen, *Commentary on the Song of Songs*. Quoted in Scheffczyk, *Faith in Christ and the Worship of Christ*, 83.

11. William H. Shannon, *Thomas Merton's Paradise Journey: Writings on Contemplation* (Cincinnati, Ohio: St. Anthony Messenger Press, 2000), 256.

12. *The Autobiography of Saint Margaret Mary* (Rockford, Ill.: Tan Books, 1986), §52, p. 67.

13. Gertrude of Helfta, *The Herald of Divine Love*, trans. Margaret Winkworth (New York/Mahwah, N.J.: Paulist Press, 1993), 99-100.

14. *Vita Christi* II, 64 (Paris 1865), 677b. Quoted in Scheffczyk, *Faith in Christ and the Worship of Christ*, 87-88.

15. Bernard of Clairvaux, *Song of Songs III*, 143. Quoted in Scheffczyk, *Faith in Christ and the Worship of Christ*, 89.

16. Anonymous Carthusian of the fourteenth century, in *Ancient Devotions to the Sacred Heart of Jesus by Carthusian Monks of the XIV-XVII Centuries*, 4th ed. (Westminster, Md.: The Newman Press, 1954), 21-22.

17. Orlando O. Espín, *The Faith of the People: Theological Reflections on Popular Catholicism* (Maryknoll, N.Y.: Orbis Books, 1997), xiv.

18. Bonaventure, *The Soul's Journey into God, the Tree of Life, the Life of St. Francis*, trans. Ewert Cousins (New York: Paulist Press, 1978), 155.

19. It is not known whether Helfta was part of the Cistercian Reform or not. In any case, the Cistercians, like the Benedictines, followed the same basic rule and rhythm of life.

20. Gertrude of Helfta, *The Herald of Divine Love*, 100.

21. Ibid., 102-103.

22. Ibid.

23. Ibid., 83.

24. Cf. Jean Leclerq's now classic *The Love of Learning and the Desire for God*, trans. Catharine Misrahi (New York: Fordham University Press, 1961).

25. Based on a vision of Mechthild of Hackeborn (c. 1240-1298). Speaking to Mechthild, Christ describes the cross itself as the bridal bedchamber ("thalamus") in which he consummated his love for humankind:

> You should remember how I entered the chamber of the cross: and just as the grooms give their garments to the players, so I gave my clothing to the soldiers, and my body to the crucifiers. Then I extended my arms with the hardest nails in your sweet embraces, singing to you in the chamber of love seven songs full of the most wonderful sweetness [a reference to Christ's seven last words on the cross]. After this I opened my heart so that you could enter as I, dying with you on the cross, suffered the sleep of love.

Quoted in Mechthild of Hackeborn, *Revelationis Gertrudianae ac Mechthildianae*, ed. L. Paquelin, 2 vols. (Portiers and Paris, 1875-77). I have relied on Jeffrey F. Hamburger's translation-report of Mechthild's vision found in *Nuns As Artists: The Visual Culture of a Medieval Convent* (Berkeley and Los Angeles: University of California Press, 1997), 135.

26. A group of these "Nonnenarbeiten" have survived and are the focus of the study by Jeffrey F. Hamburger, *Nuns As Artists*. Hamburger identifies the figures as the Trinity, which makes sense theologically. But, while the dove is clearly the Holy Spirit, the other figures are quite clearly a haloed young bearded male and a haloed young woman with flowing golden hair.

27. *Prayers of Catherine of Siena*, ed. Suzanne Noffke, O.P. (New York/Ramsey, N.J.: Paulist Press, 1983), 102.

28. John Chrysostom. Quoted in Stierli, *Heart of the Saviour*, 54.

29. Carolyn Walker Bynum, *Holy Feast, Holy Fast: The Religious Significance of Food to Medieval Women* (Berkeley and Los Angeles: University of California Press, 1987).

30. This account is from Raymond of Capua's *Life of Catherine*. Quoted in Bynum, *Holy Feast, Holy Fast*, 115.

31. Noffke, *Prayers of Catherine of Siena*, 102.

32. See John Dillenberger, *Images and Relics: Theological Perceptions and Visual Images in Sixteenth-Century Europe* (Oxford: Oxford University Press, 1999).

33. For a collection of such remarkable images, see N. Boyadjian, *The Heart: Its History, Its Symbolism, Its Iconography, and Its Diseases*, trans. Agnes Hall (Antwerp, Belgium: Esco Books, 1985).

34. "The Heart of Matter," in Teilhard de Chardin, *The Heart of Matter*, trans. R. Hogue (London, 1978), 42, 44.

35. Augustine, *Confessions*, trans. R. S. Pine-Coffin (London: Penguin Books, 1961), 134, 151.

36. Pascal, *Pensées*, trans. A. J. Krailsheimer (London: Penguin Books, 1995), 9-11.

37. Paul Avis, *God and the Creative Imagination: Metaphor, Symbol, and Myth in Religion and Theory* (London and New York: Routledge, 1999).

38. For an excellent treatment of Lynch on faith, see Gerald L. Bednar, *Faith As Imagination: The Contribution of William F. Lynch, S.J.* (Kansas City, Mo.: Sheed and Ward, 1996).

39. Ibid., 54.

40. William F. Lynch, "Theology and the Imagination," *Thought* 29/112 (Spring 1954), 66. Quoted in Bednar, *Faith As Imagination*, 58.

41. Text: Wendy M. Wright; tune: Kevin Vogt. © 2000.

42. Cf. Wendy M. Wright, "'That Is What It Is Made for': The Image of the Heart in the Spirituality of Francis de Sales and Jane de Chantal," in *Spiritualities of the Heart: Approaches to Personal Wholeness in Christian Tradition*, ed. Annice Callahan, R.S.C.J. (New York: Paulist Press, 1990), 144. See also, John A. Abruzzese, *The Theology of Hearts in the Writings of St. Francis de Sales* (Rome: Pontifical University of St. Thomas Aquinas, 1983).

43. Gentleness is the defining "little virtue" of the Salesian tradition but Jane de Chantal spoke and wrote a great deal about simplicity and developed that concept beyond Francis's thought. See Wendy M. Wright, "Jane de Chantal on Simplicity," *Salesian Living Heritage* (Spring/Fall 1989), 4-15.

44. See Terence A. McGoldrick, *The Sweet and Gentle Struggle: Francis de Sales on the Necessity of Spiritual Friendship* (New York: University Press of America, 1996).

45. St. Francis de Sales, *Selected Letters*, trans. Elisabeth Stopp (New York: Harper & Bros., 1960), 193.

46. This story first appeared in Wendy M. Wright, *The Time Between: Cycles and Rhythms in Ordinary Time* (Nashville, Tenn.: Upper Room Books, 1999), 212-218.

47. Text: William H. How, 1823-97.

48. Adapted from John Eudes, "Meditations for the Feast of the Sacred Heart of Jesus," *The Sacred Heart of Jesus by Saint John Eudes*, trans. Dom. Richard Flower, O.S.B. (New York: Kenedy and Sons, 1946), 85-110.

49. Ibid., 96.

50. Adapted from John Eudes, "Other Meditations on the Sacred Heart," in Flower, *The Sacred Heart of Jesus by Saint John Eudes*, 121-122.

51. See Ted A. Campbell, *The Religion of the Heart: A Study of European Religious Life in the Seventeenth and Eighteenth Centuries* (Columbia, S.C.: University of South Carolina Press, 1991).

52. Johann Arndt, *True Christianity*, trans. Peter Erb (New York: Paulist Press, 1979), 224.

53. Gary R. Sattler, *God's Glory, Neighbor's Good: A Brief Introduction to the Life and Writings of August Hermann Francke* (Chicago: Covenant Press, 1982), 31.

54. Nicolas Ludwig, Count von Zinzendorf, quoted in *Pietists: Selected Writings*, ed. Peter C. Erb (New York: Paulist Press, 1983), 308-310.

55. Arthur J. Freeman, *An Ecumenical Theology of His Heart: The Theology of Count Nicholas Ludwig von Zinzendorf* (Bethlehem, Pa.: The Moravian Church of America, 1998), 193.

56. Quoted in Campbell, *The Religion of the Heart*, 119.

57. A. Vermeersch, S.J., *Practical Devotion to the Sacred Heart*, trans. Madame Cecilia (New York: Benziger Bros., 1909), 16-17.

58. Text: Wendy M. Wright; tune: Kevin Vogt. © 2000.

59. Karen Armstrong, *A History of God: The 4,000 Year Quest of Judaism, Christianity, and Islam* (New York: Ballantine Books, 1993), 317-318.

60. *Vie et oeuvres de Sainte Marguerite Marie*, presentation by Professor R. Darricau (Paris-Fribourg: Editions St. Paul, 1991), 1:82-84. Margaret Mary recorded several versions of this revelation. This is the one found in her autobiography. For the various versions, see E. Glotin, "Un jour de Saint Jean l' Evangeliste', les differentes recits d'une mème apparition," in *Saint Marguerite-Marie et le message de Paray-le-Moniale*, ed. R. Darricau and B. Peyrous (Paris: Editions Desclée, 1993), 291-322.

61. *The Autobiography of Saint Margaret Mary*, trans. the Sisters of the Visitation (Rockford, Ill.: Tan Books, 1986), 69-70.

62. Croiset wrote what was to become the first biography of Margaret Mary as an appendix to his *On the Devotion to the Sacred Heart*, published in 1691. Gallifet for a while was under the spiritual direction of Claude de la Colombière. His writing pleaded for the establishment of a feast for the Sacred Heart.

63. *Autobiography*, 113.

64. Ibid., 106-107.

65. See Jacques Le Brun, "Politics and Spirituality: Devotion to the Sacred Heart," in *The Concrete Christian Life*, ed. C. Duqouc (New York: Herder, 1971), 29-43.

66. Dag Hammarskjöld, *Markings*, trans. Leif Sjöberg and W. H. Auden (New York: Alfred A. Knopf, 1965), 214.

67. *Margaret Ebner: Major Works*, trans. Leonard P. Hindsley (New York/Mahwah, N.J.: Paulist Press, 1993), 49.

68. "Coeurs (Échange des)," in *Dictionnaire de Spiritualité ascetique et mystique*, ed. Marcel Viller (Paris: Beauchesne, 1937-), 2:1048-1051. On Catherine, see Sr. Mary Jeremiah, O.P., *The Secret of the Heart: A Theological Study of Catherine of Siena's Teaching on the Heart of Jesus* (Front Royal, Va.: Christendom Press, 1995).

69. A version of this discussion was first given as a talk, "The Sacred Heart and Violence Today," at the Conference of Sacred Heart Communities in Collaboration, Loyola University, Chicago, Ill., June 26-29, 1997.

70. Julian of Norwich, *Showings*, trans. and intro. Edmund College, O.S.A., and James Walsh, S.J. (New York: Paulist Press, 1978), 298.

71. Catherine of Siena, quoted in Suzanne Noffke, O.P., "Catherine of Siena: Responsive Heart," in Callahan, *Spiritualities of the Heart*, 70.

72. Pierre Teilhard de Chardin, quoted in Ursula King, *The Life and Vision of Teilhard de Chardin* (Maryknoll, N.Y.: Orbis Books, 1996), 226.

73. Sister Margaret, quoted in Flower, *The Sacred Heart of Jesus by Saint John Eudes*, 63.

74. *Oeuvres de Saint François de Sales*, complete edition (Annecy: Monastère de la Visitation, 1892-1964), 3:216-217.

75. "Entretiens," in Sainte Jeanne-Françoise Frémyot de Chantal, *Sa Vie et ses oeuvres*, vol. 2, *Oeuvres diversès* (Paris: E. Plon, 1875), 318. The translation is mine.

76. William of St. Thierry, quoted in *Bønnebok for den katolske kirke* (Prayer book of the Catholic Church of Norway), trans. Susanne A. Koch, 283.

77. On Margaret Mary as part of the tradition of "Victim Souls," see Marie J. Willis, *Margaret Mary Alacoque: A Study of Suffering in the Life of a Victim Soul*, master's degree thesis, University of Kansas, 1991.

78. Margaret Mary Alacoque, quoted in Emile Bougaud, *The Life of Saint Margaret Mary Alacoque* (Rockford, Ill.: Tan Books, 1990), 116.

79. On this theme see Wendy M. Wright, "Jane de Chantal and the Martyrdom of Love: An Exploration of a Theme," in *Salesian Insights*, ed. William C. Marceau, C.S.B. (Bangalore, India: SFS Publications, 1999), 13-28.

80. Etienne Catta, *La Vie d'un monastère sous l'ancien régime: La Visitation Sainte-Marie Nantes (1630-1792)* (Paris: J. Vrin, 1954), 465-66. Quoted in *I Leave You My Heart: A Visitandine Chronicle of the French Revolution: Mother Marie Jeronyme Verot's Letter of 15 May 1794*, trans. Péronne-Marie Thibert, V.H.M. (Philadelphia, Pa.: St. Joseph's University Press, 1999), 15-16.

81. The fascinating tale of the Sacred Heart and the French monarchy is told in detail in Raymond Jonas, *France and the Cult of the Sacred Heart: An Epic Tale for Modern Times* (Berkeley and Los Angeles: University of California Press, 2000).

82. Cf. Thibert, *I Leave You My Heart*, 45ff.

83. Pius XII, *Haurietis Aquas*, §34.

84. A summary of these specifications as summarized by Jean Bainvel is found in the 1910 *Catholic Encyclopedia*, vol. 7 (www.newadvent.org/cathen/07163a.htm).

85. See *Mexican Devotional Retablos from the Peters Collection*, ed. Joseph F. Chorpenning, O.S.F.S (Philadelphia, Pa.: St. Joseph University Press, 1994); and Institute of Contemporary Art, Boston, catalogue from the exhibition *El Corazon Sangrante: The Bleeding Heart* (Seattle, Wash.: University of Washington Press, 1991).

86. *Prayers and Practice in the American Community*, ed. Joseph Chinnici and Angela Dries (Maryknoll, N.Y.: Orbis Books, 2000), 6ff.

87. *Letters of Saint Frances Xavier Cabrini*, trans. Sr. Ursula Infante, M.S.C. (Chicago: Archdiocese of Chicago, 1970), 420.

88. Ibid., 426.

89. Ibid., 454.

90. Ibid., 465.

91. Ibid., 115.

92. Karen Armstrong, "The God of All Faiths," telecast "God at 2000," sponsored by Trinity Institute, February 12, 2000.

93. Catherine of Siena, *The Dialogue*, trans. Suzanne Noffke, O.P. (New York: Paulist Press, 1980), 60-62.

94. Alphonsus de Liguori, *Selected Writings*, ed. Frederick M. Jones, C.SS.R. (New York: Paulist Press, 1999), 231.

95. Roger A. Bullard, *Messiah: The Gospel according to Handel's Oratorio* (Grand Rapids, Mich.: Eerdmans, 1993), 67.

96. Cf. Jeanne Weber, O.S.B., "Devotion to the Sacred Heart: History, Theology, and Liturgical Celebration," *Worship* 72/3 (May 1998), 236-254; and Richard Gutzwiller, "Notes on Some Official Texts of the Church's Devotion to the Sacred Heart," in Stierli, *Heart of the Saviour*, 157-172.

97. Pius XII, *Haurietis Aquas*, §§55, 60.

98. Pierre Teilhard de Chardin, unpublished journal 6, quoted in Faricy, "The Heart of Christ in the Writings of Teilhard de Chardin," in Callahan, *Spiritualities of the Heart*, 183.

99. Text: Wendy M. Wright; music: Martin Willett. © 2000. Inspired by the writings of Pierre Teilhard de Chardin.

100. On Rahner, see Annice Callahan, R.S.C.J., *Karl Rahner's Spirituality of the Pierced Heart: A Reintepretation of Devotion to the Sacred Heart* (Lanham, Md.: University of America Press, 1985). See also, Karl Rahner, "Some Theses on the Theology of the Devotion," in Stierli, *The Heart of the Saviour*, 131-155.

101. On Teilhard, see Robert Faricy, S.J., "The Heart of Christ in the Writings of Teilhard de Chardin," in Callahan, *Spiritualities of the Heart*, 170-185.

102. Ibid.

103. Quoted in Christopher F. Mooney, *Teilhard de Chardin and the Mystery of Christ* (Garden City, N.Y.: Doubleday Image, 1968), 28-29.

104. Pierre Teilhard de Chardin, *The Prayer of the Universe: Selected from Writings in Time of War* (New York: Harper & Row, 1968), 103-104.

105. Francis de Sales, in *The Sermons of St. Francis de Sales for Advent and Christmas*, trans. the Nuns of the Visitation, ed. Fr. Lewis S. Fiorelli, O.S.F.S. (Rockford, Ill.: Tan Books, 1987), 71-72. Adaptation by Fr. Joseph Power, O.S.F.S.

106. Francis de Sales, *Introduction to the Devout Life*, trans. John K. Ryan (Garden City, N.Y.: Doubleday Image Books, 1972), 184.

107. I am indebted to Fr. Joseph Chorpenning, O.S.F.S., for his research on this motif presented in the Salesian Scholars Seminar in 2000. Chorpenning's paper, "'You Have Engraved Ny Name in Your Heart': St. Francis de Sales' 'Portrait of the Sacred Heart of Jesus,'" was first delivered as an address in Philadelphia. He and I draw upon Eric Jager, *The Book of the Heart* (Chicago: Chicago University Press, 2000).

108. Charles Wesley, "O For a Heart to Praise My God" (1742).

109. Francis de Sales, in *The Sermons of St. Francis de Sales for Lent*, trans. the Nuns of the Visitation, ed. Fr. Lewis Fiorelli, O.S.F.S. (Rockford, Ill.: Tan Books, 1987), 62.

110. Text: Wendy M. Wright; music: Martin Willett.